D0809436

IN THE MIDST OF OUR WORLD

Forces of Spiritual Renewal

PAUL JOSEF CORDES

IN THE MIDST
OF OUR WORLD

Forces of Spiritual Renewal

TRANSLATED BY

PETER SPRING

IGNATIUS PRESS   SAN FRANCISCO

Title of the German original:
Mitten in unserer Welt:
Kräfte geistlicher Erneuerung
© 1987 byVerlag Herder GmbH & Co., KG,
Freiburg im Breisgau

Cover by Roxanne Mei Lum

With ecclesiastical approval
© 1988 Ignatius Press, San Francisco
ISBN 0-89870-208-9
Library of Congress catalogue number 88-81093
Printed in the United States of America

To all fellow-helpers
and volunteers at the
San Lorenzo International
Youth Center in Rome

CONTENTS

INTRODUCTION

Pope John Paul II chose as the theme of the Synod of Bishops 1987 the "Vocation and Mission of the Laity in the Church and in the World, Twenty Years after the Second Vatican Council". In the preparation of this convocation of the world's episcopate, it became clear that the postconciliar period has witnessed an astonishing upsurge of spiritual forces in the Church.

The climate of the synod itself was determined precisely by the discussions on ecclesial movements. The Synod Assembly, to tell the truth, dwelt less on those associations and groups that already have a well-consolidated experience. The discussion of the new realities of Catholic associations or movements was a different story.

The numerous interventions, made in this regard by the Fathers and the laity in plenary sessions and in the language groups, focused attention more and more on this conciliar and postconciliar phenomenon. Never before had the new ecclesial realities so deeply engaged their supreme leaders. And, if we consider the important role that synods have, in principle, in the orientations of the Church, we must certainly speak of an epoch-making step. All this is a sign of the importance attributed to them throughout the world. It is worthwhile, therefore, to treat these movements in more detail, especially with regard to their pastoral aspect and their theological inspiration.

Since 1979 the Pontifical Council for the Laity has invited men and women lay leaders in all continents, together with their pastors, to a series of meetings that have served a useful role both for the exchange of views and for more effective cooperation in the field of the lay apostolate. These meetings, like many other contacts and discussions, have shown that new spiritual ferments are to be felt in many local churches: those that have evidently reacted more promptly and sensitively to contemporary processes and the feelings of people in our time, and perhaps also those who ecclesial structures have not stood in the way of the new lay movements or at least have restricted them less. In any case, the phenomenon of the new spiritual ferments needs to be thoroughly examined, not only with a view to its theological elucidation and greater stability, but more especially because the spiritual movements make a contribution to the fulfillment of the Church's mission that can hardly be overestimated. Why this should be so can briefly be outlined.

1. Our faith in God is characterized by the greater trust and fidelity we display in our daily life. Yet this sense of trust in our familiar everyday

life is deepened as soon as God goes beyond the familiar impulses of ordinary Christian life and places signs of his presence "in the midst of our world". Someone who has concluded that God, as a result of his sometimes painful silence, is a distant, unapproachable being, then discovers to his surprise that if we give ourselves to God, he awakens new life in us through the Holy Spirit. New joy in the Gospel leads to a new willingness to help each other and serve the Church and our fellowmen. This dedication and commitment on behalf of all our fellowmen, assumed in diversity and unity, bring those who are seeking and those alienated from God to the realization: "God is among you indeed" (1 Cor 14:25).

2. This certainty of God's presence among us becomes all the more crucial in the face of the experience of the various criticisms leveled against the Church and also in the face of the questions posed by her own members and modern man about meaning and mission. Quite clearly the various new spiritual movements that have emerged in our time build bridges capable of closing the temporal gap between the salvific deeds of Jesus and our unredeemed age. Through concrete impulses of Christian piety and corresponding forms of Christian praxis, they offer relevant aids for the pursuit of the faith in our time. Revelation is given an appealing face, once again inviting us to action. Thanks to the spiritual movements, moreover,

the Gospel is constantly rejuvenated; it leads to personal meeting with the Lord and, through imitation of him, to dedication to the Father.

3. Christians who bear witness to God's living presence among us cannot avoid involving themselves in the world and exposing themselves to its power. For the Good News of Jesus demands that it be proclaimed "from the housetops" (Mt 10:27); it is not something to be hoarded for private edification. And the urge to spread the Good News becomes all the stronger the more the individual is moved by the truth of the Faith: "Woe to me if I do not preach the gospel!" (1 Cor 9:16).

Spiritual movements have quite unjustifiably been accused of esoteric isolation and apostolic sterility. Yet since the Council they have quite demonstrably prepared the ground for the seed of the Word of God among men in many parts of the world. Since the Gospel is for them the password to a new, hitherto undiscovered land, they "cannot but speak" (Acts 4:20) of what they have seen and heard. This commitment leads them to speak up for social justice and peace among peoples— even if the means to the achievement of these ends are sought not in political action but by individual conversion: by the conversion of the human heart. Contributions to the transformation of society and the state are thus in no way lacking in the spiritual movements. Moreover, well-informed reports on their various initiatives and plans show that these groups are a good deal less unworldly than they are sometimes accused of being.

4. Service to the Church and to society must be directed by each spiritual community at the particular church to which it belongs. A movement's special spiritual endowment absolves neither it nor its individual members from their duties to the parish or other significant Church structures. The diocese and parish form the basic ecclesial structures within which Christian faith and action are appropriately centered: it is in them that our "neighbor" lives; and it is in them that the "hour of truth", the proof of quality, are to be looked for. Otherwise, membership of a spiritual movement—and *engagement* on its behalf—would simply become a form of escape; it would weaken rather than strengthen the ability to lead a Christian life.

It is therefore important to make known the ways in which this mission can be ever more effectively performed to the benefit of the local church and its community. Trust between the members of the movements and their appointed pastor, and mutual deference between them, are thus unvoidable. Only on this assumption will all in common discover the spiritual values and forces capable of being devoted to the service of the community. The members of the movements in fact do make themselves available for particular pastoral tasks: religious instruction for children, adolescents and adults, the encouragement of spiritual activities among members, the arrangement of liturgies and the Divine Offices, concern for religious vocations or the undertaking of charitable and social activities all proclaim "what the Spirit says to the churches" (Rev 2:7–11).

To ensure that concrete action enduringly preserves its theological and spiritual depth, it is in many places accompanied by formative and educational activities. This conceals a twofold dynamic. First, these activities provide the experience that each community must continuously commit itself to the particular task for which it was originally set up; otherwise the fullness of the Church's charisms cannot be preserved intact. At the same time, however, it is essential that each group and the cultivation of its spirituality be geared to the patrimony of the Faith as a whole; only in this way can they preserve unity in diversity.

This very rapid review would like to convince sceptics too that the Council has borne abundant fruits. It emphasizes the fact that baptized Christians must be treated, not as the recipients but as the bearers of the Gospel message, guided and sanctified by the Holy Spirit.

Pope John Paul II writes in his most recent encyclical, dedicated to the Mother of the Redeemer, that he is pleased to note that in our own time new manifestations of Marian spirituality and devotion are not lacking (*Redemptoris Mater*, no. 48). He could also mean by this the new spiritual movements that have a kind of common denominator in their inner relationship to Mary. Indeed, it is in this Marian devotion that the deepest source of their missionary dynamic lies. For Mary is hailed as the Queen of the Apostles: "As a mother she also wishes the messianic power of her Son to be manifested, that salvific power of his which is meant to help man in his misfortunes, to free him from the evil which in various forms and degrees weighs heavily upon his life" (ibid., no. 21).

Bishop Paul Josef Cordes
Vice President
Pontifical Council for the Laity

I

NEW SPIRITUAL FERMENTS
IN THE CHURCH

The so-called spiritual movements ought to be sure of receiving heightened attention in our time. Whoever takes a closer look at them soon notes, however, that they cannot rightly be conveyed by a balanced, encyclopedic review. A far better idea of them can be given by a description, examination and interpretation of some concrete phenomena of Church life. Such a method will also be more likely to preserve their particular coloration and appeal than would a merely factual and correspondingly distanced account.

The danger of such an approach is of course that it may give rise to a one-sided accentuation. And I feel bound right at the outset to confess to some partisanship: I am convinced of the great significance of the spiritual movements for the proclamation of the Gospel in our time, and would also like to justify this conviction. Moreover, I would like to win others to it. My endeavors to do so will not fly in the face of the truth, but will have as their consequence a deliberate emphasis on the positive sides of the movement.[1]

[1] On the question of the spiritual movements and the

My account of the spiritual movements is in any case based on my eight years' activity within the Pontifical Council for the Laity in Rome, the office of the Holy See responsible for these new ecclesial communities at the Vatican level.

1. Brief Description of the Spiritual Movements

Many aspects of the spiritual movements are worth describing. First, their organization and structure: the fact that in spite of strong readiness for change, they place such emphasis on an unusual degree of coherence and fidelity to the charisms with which they were founded. A second aspect worth stressing is the great effectiveness by which they are distinguished, in spite of the virtual absence of full-time office-holders from their ranks. A third remarkable factor is their strong financial position, which is achieved in many movements despite the absence of any obligatory or controlled system of contributions or levies. Fourth, we may note their efficient sys-

---

problems they have given rise to, see the author's further contributions: *Neue geistliche Bewegungen in der Kirche*, issued by the Press Office of the Archdiocese of Cologne (*Zeitfragen* 31), 1985; and "Geistliche Bewegungen als Chance für die Jugendpastoral", in *Internationale katholische Zeitschrift* (1983), 457–64.

tem of communication, which succeeds in covering their often huge territorial extension.

All these factors provide supports for these groups that are not to be underestimated and that make a notable contribution to the spiritual revival in the Church in our time. Yet in the understanding of the movements themselves they are not of primary importance: they are at the service of something else. For the decisive motive for the leaders and members of these movements consists in spreading the Faith through winning over others to the goals of the particular movement they represent; this apostolic commitment goes hand in hand with an ecclesial consciousness that is never seriously threatened.

It seems reasonable to begin our account by describing objectively the individual movements and statistically quoting the number of their members. Yet it has to be said that precise figures about their membership are hard to come by—not least because the movements themselves attach little value to bureaucratic methods and administrative procedures. Yet to give at least a rough idea, I would like to cite a selection of these movements.

At Rocca di Papa (near Rome) in May 1983, the Pontifical Council for the Laity held the third joint meeting of the lay movements with which it has regular contacts. Of the groups present at this meeting, the following could be described as spiritual movements:

Apostolic Movement of Schönstatt
Christian Life Communities
Communion and Liberation
Community of Sant'Egidio
Cursillo Movement
Equipes Notre Dame
Foi et Lumière
Knights of the Immaculata
L'Arche
Legion of Mary
Marriage Encounter
Movement for a Better World
Oasis Movement
Opus Dei
"Pro Sanctitate" Movement
Secular Fraternity of Charles de Foucauld
Society of St. Francis de Sales,
    Apostleship of Prayer
Society of St. Vincent de Paul
Theresian Institution[2]

In addition, brief description of three of the numerically biggest spiritual movements in our time will make it abundantly clear that these groups can in no way be regarded as peripheral or marginal phenomena of the Catholic Church.

[2] For more detailed information on these lay associations, see Pontifical Council for the Laity, *Lay Associations, Summary Data* (Vatican City, 1983).

1. *Catholic Charismatic Renewal.* Founded in the U.S.A. in 1967, the movement's burgeoning prayer groups now comprise approximately 15 million faithful all over the world, with some 5 to 7 million in the U.S.A. alone. In some regions these prayer groups include more strictly controlled and rigorously disciplined communities akin to religious orders: these are the so-called covenant communities, with a total of about 35,000 members.

2. *The Focolarini Movement.* Founded by Chiara Lubich at Trent in Italy in 1943, this international movement has now spread to 146 nations around the world. It is still presided over by Chiara Lubich, who writes a monthly biblical meditation called *Word of Life.* The dissemination of this monthly meditation provides some quantitative indication about the strength of the movement and the scale of its influence. The *Word of Life* is published: in the form of 1,200,000 leaflets; through 1,250,000 reprints in newspapers; and through broadcasts by 102 radio stations and 5 television channels. It is translated into a total of 43 languages, including languages for the blind.

3. *The Neocatechumenal Movement.* A survey of the movement conducted in December 1985 accounted for 7,187 communities in 2,568 parishes. Since each community comprises some thirty to

forty members, the movement's total membership can be estimated at around 250,000.

Hans Urs von Balthasar, one of the most alert and perceptive observers of spiritual trends in the Church internationally and one of the leading authorities on spirituality in our time, wrote in a position paper for the Pontifical Council for the Laity in 1982:

> Not until our own century do we see the spread of such a flourishing variety of self-sufficient lay movements in the Church. While some of these can undoubtedly continue to draw their inspiration from the major charisms of the past, the majority of them have in fact sprung from new and original impulses of the Holy Spirit.

The reasons for the rapid and enduring expansion of these new realities in the Church have been analyzed in many places. Prominent among them is a psychological analysis of the mentality of contemporary man, his need for community, his hunger not only to hear the content of the Good News but also if possible to experience it. These are the factors that have been stressed in explaining why the spiritual movements have had so strong an impact on people and so positive an effect on Christian life and culture, weakened by secularism in many places. Undoubtedly these anthropological elements are more markedly present in the movements than in the local Church community—

more markedly, it has to be admitted, than is even possible for the pastoral ministry in the parishes.

At any rate, a pastor who wants to learn from the spiritual movements how to carry out his own pastoral ministry is more likely to be frustrated than helped by the psychological insights I have mentioned: he cannot easily change the parish structure. Yet, happily, psychology alone does not go far enough if one wants to explain the penetration of the spiritual movements. For it seems that their success is based not on an intelligent insight into and empathy with today's mentality alone, but also on a willingness to take seriously a few central theological tenets. Indeed, it sometimes seems to me that qualified members of the spiritual movements live their faith in a more radical fashion than do most Christians.

Reflection on the new spiritual ferments in the Church can in this way provide an inducement to the day-to-day pastoral ministry of the Church and enable it to be newly illuminated by the spiritual movements. In assessing why this should be so, the value that these movements attribute to the Word of God should first be considered.

2. The Word of God— Its Status and Communication

God's revelation has not preserved its identity unscathed through the course of history. Its integ-

rity has often been threatened, its truth obscured.
Even in the Bible itself this danger is recognized:
the warning is made against "turning to a different
gospel" (Gal 1:6), and the need recognized to
guard the truth entrusted to the faithful (see for instance 2 Tim 1:12ff.). It seems reasonable, therefore, that we in our time should not uncritically
accept the current interpretation of the Gospel in
letter and spirit but should subject it to renewed
scrutiny.

Here, however, my attention will not be directed at individual substantial contents of the
Gospel. Rather, I would like to address myself, at
least summarily, to Revelation in general and the
way in which it is understood. The elucidation of
this question can also help explain something
about the dynamic of the spiritual movements.

1. Ever since antiquity, the relation of man to
the absolute has been the object of constant investigation. But it is only in modern times that the
question has been systematically tackled in the
context of the academic disicpline of "comparative religious studies".

Initially, Christianity was attacked by this new
academic discipline, but later it too was incorpo-
rated into the curriculum and thus came to be re-
valued in a quite new context: that of comparative
religion. Today, we cannot fail to acknowedge
that the teachings on man purveyed in the academic study of religion have also proved be-

neficial to the preaching of the Christian Faith, for instance, in revealing the weaknesses of a materialistic mentality and every kind of worldly euphoria.

On the other hand, it also has to be admitted that bringing our Faith into line with the other religions and equating it with them, which the study of comparative religion entails, create new problems: they tend to obscure among many people the fact that God's Revelation is unique. For we would be doing it an injustice were we to reduce it to just one of the many articulations of the human quest for the meaning of life. Rather, the Revelation is something uniquely given to man; it claims exclusive authority; it is "living and active, sharper than any two-edged sword" (Heb 4: 12). An obvious difficulty therefore arises: How is it possible even to conceive of, never mind submit to, the claims to absolutism of God's Word in the context of one of the disciplines associated with the academic study of religion, such as its history, philosophy, phenomenology, sociology or psychology?

2. The same suspicion of a possible weakening of the identity of the Gospel message (is it perhaps the consequence of the development I have just mentioned?) arises with regard to the present-day understanding of religious instruction in schools, an issue of even greater actuality in our time. Again, the problem is how to ensure the recogni-

tion of the content of the Revelation in a determined social context, for the new understanding of religious instruction has indeed grown out of this commendable purpose.

What is meant here can be more easily grasped by considering a concrete issue: for instance, the discussions and final resolutions of the Würzburg Synod in the Federal Republic of Germany. Restricted to a particular social context, the Church has been forced to make concessions on the claims of the Word of God. Thus, the term *catechesis*—the instruction of schoolchildren in the knowledge and practice of the Faith and their preparation for religious maturity—was studiously avoided in the Synod's final resolutions. The teaching of the Faith and conviction in the faith now seem an idea that is seldom attainable. Yet precisely for this reason the Church should see religious instruction as an urgent and rewarding task, because the hope is that by means of it pupils "on leaving school will at least not consider religion and faith superfluous or even nonsensical"; that they may "conceive of religion and faith as a possible enrichment of man, as a possible force for the development of his personality and as a possible impetus for the realization of freedom"; that they may have "achieved respect for the convictions of others" (Resolution on "Religious Instruction" 2.5.6).

Certainly, it cannot be denied that a combination of fundamental legislation, political concession and educational science has significantly narrowed the scope for the achievement of the goals of religious instruction. Yet the Church's own self-limitation, as exemplified above, cannot be cause for satisfaction either. It smacks of resignation. And the risk is that what was once thought of as a possible and unavoidable exception will become the rule. Religious education, in short, will be reduced to a distanced, pseudo-objective information *about* the contents of the Faith, and will exclude in a quite unpedagogic way the relevance of faith in the community and in the world.

Yet it can be shown precisely by arguments based on the findings of educational science that learning concepts essentially reduced to the cognitive level are to be rejected. A sports teacher who only discusses handball in class but never plays it with his pupils, a music teacher who merely talks about music but never makes music with his pupils, is hardly worthy of the name. In the last analysis, the relationship to sport or to music taught in the classroom must be aimed at the goal of retaining its appeal for the pupil outside the classroom, both now and in the future.

At the level of the pedagogy of religion, many experiences in recent years have enforced the notion that existential perplexity and religious conviction, and the social experience and relevance of the great themes of the Faith, can profitably be expounded in religious instruction. For in this way many of man's perceptive faculties are brought into play and the boredom of a more distanced approach avoided. Education at school in all subjects is aimed, after all, at leading pupils eventually to make their own decisions: for instance, the study of civics will lead them to decide for democracy and against dictatorship, or biology will lead them to decide for the protection and not the destruction of the environment. Religious instruction, by the same token, should be aimed at leading them to decide for the worship of God and not of idols. It follows that to ignore decisions about faith as the objective of religious instruction is something to be avoided even on pedagogical grounds.

The Apostolic Exhortation *Catechesi Tradendae* of Pope John Paul II of October 16, 1979 (in which, incidentally, no opposition between religious instruction and catechesis is admitted), states with unmistakable clarity: "The definitive aim of catechesis is to put people not only in touch but in communication, intimacy, with Jesus Christ" (no. 5).

For God's Word is not intended to be compromised or eroded by concessions. Heinrich Schlier, who devoted his life resolutely to this Word, asserts:

> In God's Word we come across a solemn public declaration, a clarion call, a proclamation that is cried out aloud. Through the Gospel we have become a forum, before which responsible witness

is given, and which challenges us to make a decision, and provokes us to adopt a stance. We hear in it a "rumor" which is not of course called so because what it announces is uncertain, but because it is the call, the "cry"of the one who is heard. . . . Christ's presence in the Word is the presence of the one speaking to us. The claim made by his presence does not arise subsequently and, so to say, additionally in the Word, so that this Word could be primarily understood in a different way. . . . The claim made in the Word is the way of his—Christ's—presence in it. It is in the Word that his *kyriotes* is given expression.[3]

Even if these sentences are not familiar to the founders of the spiritual movements, there is no doubt that they accord well with their mission. For a universal criterion of these groups in the Church is the high respect in which they hold the Word of God. They trust in it. They do not believe that it must first be "tamed" before it can speak to man. "This book works", cried a member of Charismatic Renewal, brandishing the Bible in one hand, in Ann Arbor, after he had related many events in the life of his twelve-member family.

Consider the "Word of Life" in the Focolarini movement, the "Lived Gospel" among the Cursillos, the "Love Letter from Holy Scripture" in

[3] Heinrich Schlier, *Wort Gottes, Eine neutestamentliche Besinnung* (Leipzig, 1959), 37, 43.

Marriage Encounter, the *Scrutatio* of the Bible of the Neocatechumenals, or the detailed proclamation of the Word of God in the community of Taizé: all these groups are convinced about the dignity, value and strength of the Word of God. It is above all from it that their apostolic effectiveness is derived. The insinuation of naïveté and fundamentalism springs all too easily to many critics' lips, and only confirms their inveterate scepticism.

3. A final example of a shift in emphasis in the transmission of the Revelation can be cited under the heading of "kerygmatic theology"; it is mentioned here because in this case too the spiritual movements provide a useful indication for the pastoral ministry of the Church.

So-called kerygmatic theology (from *kerygma*, meaning "to proclaim", "to announce") was a matter for discussion in the German-speaking countries during the 1930s. It emphasized that the Christian Gospel is not primarily a teaching, a certain number of sentences, a series of general statements of religious truth, which mesh together like cogs in a machine: it is, rather, a historical dialogue, a salvific process: the announcement of salvation in and through particular events interpreted as decisive acts of God.

Whoever primarily sees the Revelation as something that is teachable, something that has objective value, runs the risk of ignoring the fact that salvation must be a living reality in every individual human being. In this sense, the systemizing of the Faith, its reduction to a set of historical truths, obscures the kerygmatic character of the Revelation.

The transmission of the Faith in the movements better complies with the theological axiom of Saint Thomas Aquinas: "*Actus credentis non terminatur ad enuntiabile, sed ad rem*" (The act of believing ends not with its expression, but with the thing). The proclamation of the Faith in the movements is thus characterized more strongly by events than by concepts. Irrespective of their use of the Word and long before its discovery, they have in effect practiced "narrative theology". The close relationship they have with Holy Scripture has made them aware of the fact that Jesus appears in the Gospel as a narrating person. The disciples are listeners to narratives, which they disseminate by narrating them in turn, both orally and in writing. Christianity is in this sense a "narrative community", or at any rate it was such a "narrative community" before it began—for the best of reasons and the most honorable of purposes—its fight over the clarification of the concepts. Narration as a mode is closer to people's lives and has a greater effect on them than other forms of teaching. It often contains moments of personal witness. This demands a concern not to cause any kind of damage to the applicable theology. On the other hand, those catechists and preachers of the Gospel who simply repeat inherited formulae and texts must ask themselves whether they do so for reasons of orthodoxy or whether they are afraid of risking themselves in personal confession.

Personal witness is unavoidable for the transmission of the Faith. This may seem a platitude. Yet it is something that needs constantly to be enunciated anew in an age of mechanized communication. Technical aids of all kinds are not to be despised. Our pastoral ministry is full of them—ranging from handbills and placards to the carefully prepared parish letter, from stereo equipment to highly complex audiovisuals and video systems. Yet all this can be of only secondary help. The spiritual movements have the merit of realizing that it is personal witness that ignites the first spark.

It was above all the personalist thinkers, that is, those who adduce the human person as the key to central metaphysical problems, who formulated the transmission of the Faith in existential categories. One of them, the Frenchman Gabriel Marcel, was himself a convert and had a special gift for expressing in words the process that led to his discovery of faith.

On the way to faith (this was his finding) the person creates a relationship with a personal interlocuter, with a personal YOU, to whom he entrusts himself. Unquestionably it is the YOU of God

alone that can justify this trust in man. The search-
ing human being thus responds in faith to "something obscure, a silent invitation that fulfills or—
to put it differently—impels the soul, without
forcing it". This impulse seizes not only the person's intellect but his innermost being. It is more
than an invitation that places no obligation on us.
It challenges us at the deepest level of our being.
Were it just rational grounds by which I was
moved, were it just objective truths and factual
statements, then any kind of allegiance to the
Faith would remain superficial and external. I
could, in intellectual terms, conceive of them, but
would never be able to love them. And yet it is
only then, when my innermost being is seized by
faith, that it can give me an all-embracing sense of
security.[4]

A similar argument is developed by the theologian Jean Mouroux in his book *Je Crois en Toi*.[5]
For Mouroux, the Faith responds to the call of the
"three-personed" God who goes out to a person
through Christ. Christian faith is consequently, at
its deepest level, personal in structure: it is a search
for a *person*. It is participation in the personal trin-

[4] Cf. R. Aubert, *Problème de l'acte de foi* (Leuven, 1950),
615ff.

[5] Jean Mouroux, *I Believe: The Personal Structure of Faith*,
trans. Michael Turner (New York, 1959). (First published in
French under the title *Jean Crois en Toi, structure personelle de la
foi*.)

itarian life embodied and revealed in Christ. "Christian faith", Mouroux writes, "is specified in its entirety by Christ; it is participation in the life of a person, in the mystery of his death and Resurrection; thanks to this mediation it is a trinitarian faith, and a sharing in the life of the Three Persons" (p. 37).

This personal quality also holds good for the interpersonal transmission of the Faith. What is essential is, again, this *personal* quest, this orientation of a person toward a good that can only be another person. It is not by signs, however eye-catching, that we are won over; it is not the enunciation of an abstract truth that convinces us; nor is it any powerful principle that commands our assent. However important all this may be, Jean Mouroux argues, "if the soul comes gradually to interpret these signs and understand the words, if it assents more and more fully to the truths proposed, this is because through these signs, these words and these truths, it seeks and it discovers a person who calls it and to whom it replies" (p. 59).

The German sociologist F.-X. Kaufmann, in studying the transmission of the Faith, has identified "the self-interpretations of Christianity with widely recognized theorems and insights of sociology".[6] Though the term *spiritual movements*

[6] F.-X. Kaufmann, *Kirche begreifen. Analysen und Thesen zur gesellschaftlichen Verfassung des Christentums* (Freiburg, 1979), 6.

is not to be found in his book, Kaufmann points out insights and develops prerequisites that, from wholly different presuppositions, fully endorse the personalistic interpretations of the two French theologians I have cited, and which thus come astonishingly close to the practice of the spiritual movements. Indeed, many passages in Kaufmann's book can be read as a theory—this time sociologically founded—supporting the form of apostolate practiced by the movements.

Thus, Kaufmann argues that the shared learning of the teachings of the Faith must conform to the following requirements:

> The handing down of a system of meaning presupposes from a sociological point of view *personalized* social relationshiops. The adoption of values generally takes place through identification with persons or groups who are experienced as models. The transmission of Christian systems of meaning is therefore closely bound up with appropriate communicative prerequisites, which are normally best satisfied in the form of small group-type structures. Even school classes are likely to be generally too large for this purpose. It is clear, therfore, that the handing down of Christianity from one generation to the next is bound up with the formation of social groups within which the Christian body of thought can be experienced in a meaningful way (p. 142).

The author goes on to argue in the same sense:

The question is whether social situations of sufficient compactness and durability still exist today to enable personal relationships of sufficient intensity for the adoption of Christian values to be established. It is doubtful whether the normal life of the parish and religious instruction still suffice for this purpose (pp. 184f.).

It follows that the emotional cohesion and togetherness within a group are just as important as the quality of the teaching of the Faith itself. It has been ascertained by K. E. Nipkow in the evaluation of a representative survey of German students of both sexes at vocational school that the credibility of the Gospel message must be proved to these youngsters with reference to the following questions:

Does God even exist?
Did God create the world and me?
God and suffering?
What will happen after I die and what will
  become of the world?[7]

The specific dynamic of the various spiritual movements is based not least on the fact that they are able convincingly to answer these basic questions posed by young people, and they do so both in word and deed and in emotionally experienceable ways. In this way, not only is the weakening

[7] K. E. Nipkow, *Erwachsenwerden ohne Gott: Gotteserfahrung im Lebenslauf* (Munich, 1987), 88ff.

of the Christian tradition, elsewhere so evident,
stopped, but, more important, new ways of giving people access to it are opened and the Christian
vocation becomes realizable in a joyful and life-
enhancing way.

3. Society as Task

The close attention that needs, as I have stressed
above, to be given to the forging of personal relationships with a view to the transmission and
deepening of the Faith necessarily leads to a stronger inward-orientation among the members of the
spiritual movements: the greater emphasis they
place on the bonds among one another. That is
why they often incur the suspicion of sectarianism
or the charge of self-isolation. They may indeed
be capable of creating an inner climate and winning people over, but in so doing, it is alleged,
they forget the world about them.

On entering a movement, the active Christian
loses his concern for the transformation of society:
this is a charge repeatedly made, as for instance by
a group of Brazilian bishops during their *ad limina*
visit to Rome in 1985. In other countries, too, this
accusation is all too lightly made.

It has to be admitted that initial contacts with
the spiritual movements do arouse a suspicion that
these groups tend to flee from the world and seek

a haven in their own spiritual refuges. The emphasis of their commitment is placed quite evidently on the fostering of the Faith and on the specific goals of the individual community. Yet the reflex action of this approach on the Christian community at large should not be underestimated, either. Indeed, the fear sometimes expressed about the social abstinence of these groups, and their preponderant cultivation of piety, is shown on longer familiarity to be groundless. On the contrary, they reveal a selfless dedication to the world around them and an impressive willingness to perform social services.

Many examples could be cited in confirmation of this, such as the mission of the Community of Sant'Egidio. Founded by a group of students in Rome, this movement had its first headquarters in a Roman church dedicated to Saint Egidius, from where it spread outward throughout Italy and to other European countries. In Rome itself it has approximately 5,000 mainly young members, who devote themselves above all to social problems. They visit some 800 poor and elderly people in their homes; help with the education of 1,500 children and teenagers in the slum areas of the suburbs of Rome; organize the provision of 300 hot meals for the homeless twice a week; help organize group holidays and other leisure activities for youngsters; concern themselves with the medical care of gypsies, and so on. In most of these welfare services they work in liaison with the public welfare or Church authorities.

Very different from the social activity of the Sant'Egidio community is the commitment of another movement aimed at bringing Christian approaches into the public and political domain. It is called Communion and Liberation (in Italian: *Comunione e Liberazione*, abbreviated CL). Yet its social engagement, too, repudiates the false accusation that the spiritual movements tend to isolate themselves from the world and cultivate self-absorption.

This group was founded in the mid-1950s on the initiative of the Milanese priest and professor of philosophy Luigi Giussani. Today, it has some 150,000 members in twenty-two countries. Right from the outset, its members pledged themselves to the following objectives:

1. Young people are to be approached wherever they are strongly influenced by their environment—hence at school, where their mentality and culture are formed.

2. Jesus Christ is to be brought close to them as the meaning of their life and the key to the understanding of reality as a whole.

3. They are to be gathered together in Christ's name into communities, so that Christ can be lived and experienced as the center of their life.

These basic ideas have in the meantime undergone further development as the students who formed the movement's original membership have grown up. At the present time *Comunione e Liberazione* comprises the following three branches:

1. A fraternity of adults: this lay association, with papal recognition, forms the movement's backbone.

2. The *Cattolici Popolari* (People's Catholics), a loose confederation with political goals. The *Cattolici Popolari* also represents a significant force of student self-representation in the universities of Italy; after an extreme-left student predominance in the 1960s and 1970s, it has in the meantime grown to form the majority in over half the universities.

3. The *Memores Domini* branch: small Christian Life communities (of men or of women), who live in the spirit of the Evangelical Counsels.

The CL movement cannot help but impress by its extraordinarily incisive public role and social activity, responsibility for which lies exclusively in the hands of the movement's members and is thus formally excluded from any direct influence of the bishops. CL's public role is evident in the first place from its impressive publishing empire. This comprises:

1. The monthly membership bulletin *Litterae communionis*: monthly sale 60,000. It is especially devoted to the declarations and teachings of the Pope, and the life of the Church and of the movement itself, in which great value is attached to the formation of members and news about the movement's development in the world.

2. The weekly review *il sabato*, 85,000 copies. It enjoys a high reputation both within the movement and more widely as a well-informed paper of high journalistic standards. In its espousal of key issues regarding Italy and the wider world (abortion, educational problems, the plight of Vietnamese refugees, Nicaragua, South Africa, etc.), it is an influential forum of opinion.

3. The monthly magazine *30 giorni*, issued in five languages. It provides, in magazine format, positive Catholic information about important issues and events in the life of the Church at the international level. Thanks to a wide and comprehensive network of correspondents, it creates a truly "catholic" horizon.

One special initiative of CL is the so-called Meeting for Friendship Between Peoples. This week-long meeting has been held annually in Rimini since 1980. In 1986 the meeting was dedicated to the problems of communication (the theme was "Communication: Drums—Bit—

Messages"). According to *Time* magazine (August 8, 1986), some 600,000 visitors attended the meeting in an exhibition space covering 950,000 square feet. Prominent participants are not uncommon: Cardinals Lustiger from Paris, O'Connor from New York and Fresno from Santiago, the theologian Hans Urs von Balthasar, the world-famous author André Frossard and several foreign ministers of Mediterranean countries have already numbered among the guests.

One final example may be cited to show the welcome effects of the movement on both the Church and the wider world, this time the Focolarini movement. It is provided by Don Agostino Abate, a parish priest in Colombia:

> Our parish bears the name "La Miracolosa". It is situated to the south of the town of Armenia. It began its work after two districts of the town had been established in the midst of a large coffee plantation several years ago. Today there are eight such districts with a total population of 50,000.
>
> In 1983 a Marxist organization purchased an area of land within the parish in order to erect a Communist model housing-estate. A settlement of prefabricated huts with accommodation for 150 families speedily arose on the site; the inhabitants were pressed to become members of the Communist Party and to participate in the Communist-inspired community life. Whereas a town district in Colombia normally expects to be provided with a

place for religious worship, here the building erected at the center of the settlement as the driving force of the new community life was not a church but a "House of the People", and all forms of religious service were proscribed in the settlement. Although I knew that the people responsible for this ban were Marxists, I would never have thought so categorical a rejection of religion possible, especially as Colombia takes religious freedom seriously. When, as a result, a family in the village put their home at our disposal for the celebration of the Eucharist—as is normal practice with us if there is no church—I sallied forth with a glad heart to enter into contact with the settlement. But a cruel surprise awaited me: the party leaders explained that the prohibition of religious service was a law of the people and drove me away in a most disagreeable way.

What was I to do? Abandon this group of people to their fate? We discussed the matter in the parish council and saw in it a good opportunity for bearing witness to our "love for the rejected Jesus". We summoned up all our strength and tried to become one with the inhabitants of the district. We then found out that they had only made this political choice out of despair, in the direst need and from hunger. Members of the parish then befriended various inhabitants of the district; they went and visited the poor and the sick. Eventually some of them came more frequently to us and took part in our parish activities. Finally one of them became a member of our parish council as representative of the district. God formed a well-educated group of them, who then confessed themselves Christians before their Communist leaders in the "House of the People".

When the husband of a lady who was a member of the parish council died, she asked permission for a priest to be invited for the celebration of the Eucharist. And she was given permission: her faith and witness had the effect of making the leaders of the district change their strict rule.

Following this first step, a crib was erected at the center of the district at Christmas, and we began the Christmas novena there. At the same time, the Gen-Group [i.e., the Focolarini group] of the parish were able to prepare the children of the district for their First Communion. Meetings in the families followed. Finally, the people gave permission for the celebration of Holy Mass, which is now celebrated once a month, and where else but in the "House of the People"?[8]

This account may sound like a modern fairy-tale. But I myself have met Don Agostino and have no grounds to doubt him.

It remains indisputable that the vocations of Christians are various. No one should go to the opposite extreme and try to absolutize the special vocation of the movements, or claim that membership in them is the necessary condition for

---

[8] *Quaderni di Gen's* (periodical of the Focolarini) 16 (April–June 1986), 20f.

qualified Christian presence in the contemporary world.

Yet one feature common to these movements is undoubtedly a matter for astonishment in our secularized times and at variance with the pastoral methods usually used today: their social engagement is rooted in a very demanding spiritual program. And because this program takes priority over everything else, these groups run less risk of being taken in, and thus perverted, by society and its laws. They are protected from the illusion that the first priority is the development of appropriate technology, the proliferation of full-time officeholders and professionals and the growth in worldly power and resources. They insist, on the contrary, on the necessary interdependence between spiritual and secular commitment.

4. Promoters of Increased and Deepened Prayer

It is appropriate, therefore, to discuss, at least summarily, the value that the new spiritual communities attach to prayer and the kind of prayer they practice. Father Roger of Taizé remarks in one of his diary entries:

> One of the questions most put to us: Why are there so many young Europeans at Taizé? My brothers and I sometimes say to each other: we

really don't know the reason why; God will one day tell us what it is face to face in Eternity.[9]

The great popularity enjoyed by this Protestant monastic community in France is undoubtedly a measure of the priority it gives to the worship of God: the fixed celebration of the canonical hours three times a day; the form of this prayer and the appealing church space in which it takes place; the gathering of the participants; the immediacy of prayer and intercession; and last the winning and, in the postconciliar period, often style-setting melodies with which the litanies are sung—all this contributes to the particular fascination of divine worship at Taizé. Those who have had a chance to experience Taizé will be urged to speak of it. Sometimes, during the few days of their stay at Taizé, the salvific power of prayer and liturgy will be newly revealed to them. The Holy Father himself, during his visit to Taizé in October 1986, emphasized just this aspect of this small but by-now famous French locality: namely, that it is a place of prayer and silence.

Just as important as the prayer of the hours for Taizé is the shared vesperlike service every evening for the Sant'Egidio community. Since the members live scattered all over the city, they meet together in various places. Their leaders consider this religious service the centerpoint of commu-

[9] Diary of Frère Roger of Taizé, September 16, 1977.

nity life and make efforts to ensure that, as one of the movement's few binding duties, it is rigorously kept.

Further examples of the importance of prayer in the life of the spiritual movements can be cited. In 1985 I was invited to the annual Congress of the Catholic Charismatic Renewal of the U.S.A. at the University of Notre Dame, South Bend, Indiana. This congress, attended by some 10,000 participants, was also strongly imbued with the spirit of prayer. Lengthy eucharistic celebrations, prayer times, joint meditation on Holy Scripture, the receiving of the sacrament of penance—all this constituted over a third of the program. I heard in January 1986 that the members of the City of the Lord covenant community in Phoenix, Arizona, are endeavoring to establish joint neighborhoods on various streets in the town; they are buying up houses for this purpose and moving into them so as to be more closely together. They explained that in this way it was possible to pray lauds together at 6:15 in the morning before going to work.

During an evening visit to a family in Rome who belong to the Emmanuel charismatic community, I was asked to recite the evening prayer with the four children, aged between 5 and 12. I was led through the old Roman house to doors opening onto a niche in the wall. "Here the oven was once situated", the father explained. "We've converted it into our house altar." He opened the doors, switched on a lamp, and my glance fell on crucifix, image of our Lady, pictures of saints, flowers and candlesticks. Here we recited the evening prayer together, with praise and thanksgiving to God, a look back over the day that had passed and spontaneous intercessory prayers.

I was reminded of the idea of household shrines, which the founder of the Schönstatt movement, Father Josef Kentenich, developed many years ago. Shrines of our Lady are built wherever the movement exists. Thus, when he wrote from Brazil in 1948, "Take the picture of the Mother of God with you and set it up in a place of honor in your homes", he rightly emphasized the pastoral value of religious signs. Indeed, he wanted to give greater immediacy and tangibility to the Faith and to spiritual life by devoting a particular place for it in each home. Yet he combined this with a concern for apostolic irradiation. Father Kentenich writes:

> If our action be blessed, then we may assume that our houses will act as a small magnet. A power will go forth from them . . . to attract this or that person, so that our shrine in fact has a power of attraction not only for us, but also for the wider world outside. [10]

[10] Cf. E. Braunbeck, *Die Familie: Eine Hauskirche* (Vallender-Schönstatt, 1985), 171.

I experienced another example of this outward irradiation with young members of *Comunione e Liberazione*. In autumn last year I visited, at 8:00 one morning, a church close to the offices of the engineering faculty of the University of Rome, San Pietro in Vincolo. I heard a group of students reciting psalms in one of the aisles of the basilica. After their prayer I went over and spoke with the young people. They told me that they met here every morning before the beginning of their studies to pray lauds together. When I accompanied a group of them on a holiday in the Dolomites a few months ago, I was also struck by the way they pulled their psalters out of their pockets during our ascent of a mountain and prayed the Church's morning prayer together.

Lastly, I would like to report on the Neocatechumens. This initiative is in fact the youngest of the postconciliar groups. It was founded by the Spanish painter Kiko Arguello in the slums of Madrid twenty years ago. It first spread among gypsies, and is especially aimed at restoring strayed sheep to the fold.

In imitation of the early Christian catechumenate, this movement demands of its members a long process of initiation, covering several stages and eventually leading to full integration in the community. At least two meetings are held each week. To a good many modern churchmen such demands seem unreasonable, and they also contradict all the psychological laws of adult education. Yet they have been proved to work. The movement's 250,000-plus members scattered all over the world and the exemplary dedication of many of them to the task of evangelization are a convincing testimony of this.

The initiation process for joining the Neocatechumenal community consists of various stages, each concluded by a test. The leaders of the community—both priests and laymen—interview the candidates and assess whether they have reached the degree of spiritual maturity sufficient to enable them to progress to the next stage.

After a period of some six years, members are entrusted with the task of prayer service: they are presented with the psalter. The members thus honored then assume responsibility for the daily praying of lauds and vespers, the meditation on the day's Gospel reading, the reading of the texts at Matins and the practice of silent, personal prayer of the heart. This "Way", as it is known, is also a school for prayer. I once asked a long-standing member what value was attached to the adoration of the Eucharist in the Neocatechumenate. He replied that from a certain late stage in the initiatory process onward, members are obliged to hold a night-long eucharistic prayer in small groups during the week of Corpus Christi. He himself had recently done so; he valued this kind of prayer highly.

It is beyond the scope of my present purpose to describe, as I would like to, the strong Marian orientation of most of the spiritual movements. Their spiritual foundations contain the most varied means of giving concrete expression to God's closeness to man and his Gospel in the image of Mary. I much regret that I can do no more than make this assertion here, without being able to particularize it, especially as further impulses for Marian devotion could well be made in all countries throughout the world.

Last, the impulses that the spiritual movements have given to the importance, depth and scope of prayer are of the greatest value. This has been recognized by John Paul II, who notes in his encyclical *Dominum et Vivificantem* on the Holy Spirit in the life of the Church and the world of May 18, 1986: "Recent years have been seeing a growth in the number of people who, in ever more widespread movements and groups, are giving first place to prayer and seeking in prayer a renewal of their spiritual life. This is a significant and comforting sign" (no. 65).

In fact, the spiritual movements have been able to lead many Christians out of the cul-de-sac of lifeless and mechanical prayer formulae and to bring them into a more intimate union with the person of the living God. In a period in which Christians have too often been seduced by a kind of hectic Pelagian activism, a self-confident endeavor to be the agents of salvation themselves, they have, moreover, reminded us that it was God who came in the person of Jesus Christ to be our salvation himself and to give himself to us.

5. The Cost of the Spiritual Renewal

People of deep faith can be encountered in the spiritual movements. Their lives seem to be more strongly imbued by God. They accept his Word to a significant degree, and base their decisions and judgments on it. They willingly let themselves be impelled by the spirit of evangelization. Indeed, when they speak of their activities, they give the impression that their enthusiasm for the propagation of the Faith equals that of the missionary orders. Yet the young enthusiasts of the spiritual movements should not too quickly be dismissed as fanatics, for their chief motivation is not proselytism: it is basically a spirit of benevolence springing from their faith that leads them to evangelize.

They use all legitimate means for their apostolate: the witness of life, through which they make friends with their fellowmen; the celebration of the sacraments in an atmosphere of community joy; devotion to the signs of the Faith and to a religious culture that signifies its mystery; festivity of worship and not desiccated, mechanical devotion; discussion of the Faith and its claims in the language of our time; detailed exposition of the biblical message and the teaching of the Church in preaching and catechesis; the building up of a community so that God's Word may be sustained by fellow-believers; and constant prayer to God that he may open the hearts of our fellowmen.

These apostolic means may be illustrated, for instance, by the work of the Neocatechumenal communities. That the work of this group in deepening the Faith should, year after year, leave ever more palpable traces should be no cause for surprise: there is a growing desire among the laity to enable those who no longer live the Gospel in their lives, or do so only superficially, to redis-cover all its richness and all the help it can give. This is fortunate indeed, and not least for the Church in western Europe: during a short visit to Hildesheim (Germany) I was told by Bishop Homeyer that, in realistic terms, one must assume that of the total population of his diocese, in which Catholics form only 20 percent, only some 5 to 7 percent are believers. In other words, the *one* lost sheep of the Gospel has been multiplied ninety-five times! The evangelization of Europe, which Pope John Paul II has frequently mentioned in re-cent times, is urgently necessary. The idea thus suggested itself to the Neocatechumens: "We'll go to the heathens in northern Europe." The mem-bers of this movement, who are more familiar with the world's areas of poverty than most academic social reformers, know that an even greater poverty must not be forgotten: the poverty of the human spirit from which God has been expelled. They therefore wish to send single families to de-christianized suburbs or rural areas in north European countries, where they will begin a kind of pre-evangelization in liaison with the local church. Later, if necessary, the many seminarians from the community, who are now being trained, can follow up their lead.[11]

At the moment, preparation for pre-evangelization is tested by lay groups within the movement. In mid-September last year I took part in a meeting held in the Abruzzi, attended by some 650 long-standing members of the Way from Italy and France. In full freedom, entirely of their own volition, 28 married couples declared their willingness to take part in the adventure. These 28 couples have the impressive total of 105 children between them; 4 or 5 children per family are not uncommon.

In itself this abundance of children has an evangelizing character: it testifies to the hope in God as Lord of the future. At any rate, the two couples

[11] It may incidentally be mentioned here that after the international youth meeting in Rome in 1985, on the evening of Palm Sunday some 1,000 young men from all over the world met with the Holy Father in the Sistine Chapel: all of them had, in undergoing the "Camino" of the Neocatechumenals, discovered their vocation to the priesthood.

who began this experiment, respectively in northern Finland and Hamburg last year, were, by their own account, perceived and judged as such by many of the people they came into contact with.

The fathers of these pioneer families cannot in any sense be described as unemployed workers in search of a job: one is the director of the civic theatre in Bari; two are reputable architects; and the others include neurosurgeons, civil engineers, business executives and civil servants in high-ranking positions. They all, together with their families, have freely chosen to abandon their material security and social position and take to the road.

It is natural that acquaintance with these people should both disturb and hearten. Their faith is inspiring, but it involuntarily convicts us of our lack of it and of our own safe, comfortable and undemanding approach to the Faith. They preach without words that the apostolate can be no easy job with security of employment; that it demands the apostle's self-sacrifice. Clearly, they do not let themselves be led astray by a pastoral style that could be described as an "apostolate in self-preservation". Pastoral service in this sense means attempting to evangelize while remaining firmly below one's protective umbrella.

For experimentation with nuclear rods, laboratories with a particular layout are built. The scientists who conduct these experiments clearly cannot remain in the area where the radiation process takes place. They therefore do so by remote control from behind a radiation-proof screen at least three feet thick. From here they can monitor what is happening and manipulate the controls with long robot arms. These "manipulator arms" convey the manual movements of the researchers into the danger zone, while they themselves remain shielded from any contamination. Without question, the nuclear laboratory is an anti-model for evangelization. If this kind of model were increasingly to characterize the pastoral conception of the Church, the Church system could perhaps be maintained, but it would hardly succeed in restoring lost sheep to the fold.

The advance into the unexplored territory of those who stand outside the Church makes it crucially important for the missionary to risk his neck and to commit himself to the very depths of his being. And here I would like to report on a final group, which I had occasion to meet in the north Italian town of Bassano del Grappa.

Over three years ago I heard for the first time about a new spiritual ferment in the parish of Santa Croce in this town. I was told that a kind of "youth parliament" had been set up in the parish, but had spread beyond it: some 400 youngsters chose from their ranks a "mayor" and "ministers" responsible for various fields of interest to young people. Until called up for military service, young men in the parish normally participated once a week in catecheisis, which was given by selected men in the parish. The former members of the youth parliament also introduced a kind of adult education, which they themselves financed. Only later did I discover the spiritual basis of the whole venture. It consists of the "Group of Ten". The members of this group (in the meantime their number has grown to almost one hundred men and women from all walks of life and all ranks of society) would like through prayer and sacrifice to maintain their town in God's favor; in addition, they pray in particular for the sanctification of priests and bishops and the redemption of the young. The name "the Ten" derives from the biblical account of the meeting of God with Abraham (Gen 18:23ff.): Abraham wanted to find ten righteous men in the city of Sodom who did not deserve damnation. If they could be found, then God promised not to destroy the city: a first compelling indication of the Old Testament revelation of the theological truth of substitution. The men and women of Bassano want to ensure that the conditions laid down by God continue to operate so that through sacrifice and prayer they too may be included in the assent given by God to Abraham: the promise, namely, not to destroy Sodom for the sake of ten righteous.

How seriously they take this endeavor was later brought home to me by a trivial occurrence. I visited the town again. One of the members of the group, a relatively young father of three sons, a leather manufacturer by trade, gave me a lift in his car. As I knew the importance prayer has in this group, I dared to ask him whether we should recite the Rosary together. He turned to me and replied: "Yes, gladly! This will be my fourth Rosary today." Then, as if in apology, he added: "I've been a long time on the road today. I've had plenty of time for it."

The Group of Ten is based on impressive models. Its original members were young people, who adopted the idea of substitution under the spiritual guidance of their parish priest, Don Didimo. That was toward the end of World War II. In northern Italy at the time war was raging and fear of fascist reprisal had grown. Every day death struck the families and neighborhoods of the town, also among the senior members of the parish youth of Santa Croce. An extraordinary heroism, such as only young people are capable of, grew up as a result. These youngsters did not want to limit themselves to the usual intercession and atonement. Six or seven of them expressed their readiness to participate utterly and unconditionally in the redeeming action of the Lord; in very different situations and quite independently of one another, they called on the parish priest and told him that they had offered their lives as a sacrifice to God in the imitation of Christ. The parish priest wrote up their stories many years later. With tears in his eyes he pointed to the photos on the walls of his house of these young men who had made the ultimate sacrifice.

Here, for instance, is the story of Aldo dall'-Alba:

This was my last meeting with him. "No, Aldo, you cannot, you must not, you cannot offer your life to God—at any rate not for the goals of our group. I forbid you to do so with all my strength." And Aldo replied: "Does the general arouse fear in his troops? I find words in the Gospel that condemn all half-heartedness." When I saw myself assailed at the level of logic, I attacked from another direction: "Gospel or no Gospel, you must not do it. If you won't listen to any other reason, think at least of the fact that you're an only child; that your parents have only you. Don't you love them?" Aldo: "What if I do love them? But Jesus too was an only son, and his mother was alone. Will not God, who has thought of you [Father], also think of my parents? If my readiness be accepted, they will quite certainly be satisfied too." And God did accept.

And this is the story of Guido:

"I am here, Father, to talk about something very important. The war is now over and I will be spending my time teaching Latin and Greek. It is a good work, but I would like to be able to do it in a way that is truly Christian. I would like my pupils to be filled with the holy fear of God." Then, seeming as if he had already proposed too much, he added, "I'd like you to teach me how to become a saint."

"Your request is a very good one", I said. "Well, you will need to begin with meditation. You should dedicate at least a quarter of an hour each day to meditation."

He answered, "I have always meditated every morning, before hearing Mass and receiving Holy Communion, since I began as a high school student."

"Well then, I suggest you recite the Rosary every day. The Blessed Virgin always helps those who say it. Naturally, she does not favor those who may want to pray out of egotistical motives, but she helps those, like yourself, who are seeking the kingdom of God."

Guido replied, "Whenever I am on my way around, from one place to another, I'm always saying the Rosary."

"Well then, what do you want me to teach you, my dear Guido?" I responded hesitantly.

"I hope", he answered, "to be able to overcome my difficulty in coping with suffering. You understand how useful and effective it is, but the bitterness of pain bears down upon me too heavily. I do not feel I have much generosity."

"Now you're exaggerating", I said. "You know that castor oil does you good, and so, you pretend that the palate, despite the bitterness, continues to taste it as if it were sweet. And furthermore, even Jesus had a certain fear of pain.

("Father, let this chalice pass from me . . .")
However, to help you get used to the thought of
suffering (given that you know its value), get
yourself a small crucifix, and, when you can,
make the Way of the Cross with it, if only (even)
once a day."

He then put his hand into his pocket and took
out a little crucifix, and said, "From four years
ago, every day I have been accompanying Jesus on
the Way of Calvary."

I was lost for words. I had known Guido to be
a good fellow, but I had never thought of him as
quite as good as this! As he was leaving, I asked
him, "Guido, are you afraid of death?"

"No", he replied.

"That's good", I said. "I believe that you are
going to die quite soon, because you are ready for
heaven. In the event, when you get there, remember me and the Ten."

Less than forty-eight hours later, I saw my
Guido, under a bush, with his chest crushed and
his face horribly mutilated. And, as I cried, I repeated to myself, "Because, Guido, you are ready
for heaven".

These are moving stories. They leave one lost
for words. Commentary becomes redundant.
Perhaps there are those who are more irritated
than moved by them, and protest against too
much morbidness. Yet is not this same heroic attitude of the young found as early as the great Ig-

natius of Antioch (d. *ca.* 107), who wrote in his first Letter to the Romans:

> Let me be fodder for wild beasts; for through them I can reach God. I am the hay of God; the teeth of the wild beasts shall grind me to make me a pure loaf for Christ.

For Hans Urs von Balthasar this martyr bishop is the prototype for the theology of substitutions (*Stellvertretung*). The visible action of the bridal Church consists in the imitation of Christ, "who went about doing good and healing all" (Acts 10:38). Therefore the Church has an obligation for everything that serves man, including the "assumption of responsibility for the removal of injustice, . . . racial discrimination or the oppression of classes and peoples". Yet this action in the imitation of Christ does not come up against its limit where the necessary human action ends: on the contrary, having reached that point it should then gain in intensity and effectiveness in the same imitation of Christ in suffering and death; indeed, it is only then that it should enter into its decisive phase.[12]

As always in considering the Church's service and in judging her apostolate, appearances do not

---

[12] Hans Urs von Balthasar, *Theodramatik*, vol. 3, *Die Handlung* (Einsiedeln, 1980), 379–95, here 394; and idem., *Truth Is Symphonic: Aspects of Christian Pluralism*, trans. Graham Harrison (San Francisco: Ignatius Press, 1987), 152–69, 166.

enable one to recognize its real source. It was the "departure" of the Lord in his death on the Cross that obtained for us the gift of the Spirit. Our present pope has developed this insight with great theological depth and conviction in his already cited encyclical on the Holy Spirit. John Paul II writes:

> The Redemption accomplished by the Son in the dimensions of the earthly history of humanity—accomplished in his "departure" through the Cross and Resurrection—is at the same time, in its entire salvific power, transmitted to the Holy Spirit. . . . Christ's "departure" is an indispensable condition for the "sending" and the coming of the Holy Spirit.[13]

No one can leave this law of salvation behind. Those who have dedicated themselves, or wish to dedicate themselves, to the awakening of the Holy Spirit in the Church at the world level, must also submit to this Spirit, though in the certainty that this same Spirit "revealed himself especially as he who gives life: 'He who raised Christ from the dead will give life to your mortal bodies also through his Spirit which dwells in you' " (Rom 8:11) (ibid., no. 58).

[13] *Dominum et Vivificantem*, no. 11; see also no. 8, 13, 14, 24, etc.

II

FROM FRANCIS OF ASSISI TO
CHARLES DE FOUCAULD:
JESUS, THE ONE MODEL
OF CHRISTIAN LIFE

The vocations and charisms with which Jesus
Christ endows his Church are diverse. Yet their
diversity and plurality should not make us forget
that they all have their source in the same Lord.
The Apostle Paul reminds us of this: "Now there
are varieties of gifts, but the same Spirit; and there
are varieties of service, but the same Lord" (1 Cor
12:4–5).

It is the Lord himself who calls to his followers,
and who is the foundation of all spiritual vocations
in the Church. His Gospel is the basis, and the
genuineness of a vocation can be verified by being
referred back to Christ and his Word.

A famous passage from world literature may
help us to grasp what this means. It indicates the
vocation of a man in such a way that it can quite
easily be distinguished from all forms of deception
that de facto link vocation and the gift of grace to
particular ideologies and interests.

1. The Scene of Our Vocation in the Gospel

In his novel *Journal d'un Curé de Campagne* (1936), the French novelist and essayist Georges Bernanos describes, in the form of a diary, the life of a young priest who is dogged not only by illness and failure, but also by spiritual anxieties and by an overwhelming sense of discouragement and sadness. One day this young priest, prostrated by despair and grief, has one of his periodic encounters with an elder colleague, the parish priest of Torcy, who tells him:

> We're all called to the priesthood, I agree, but not always in the same way. So to get things straight I start off by taking each one of us back where he belongs in Holy Writ. It makes us a couple o' thousand years younger, but what of it? Time doesn't worry our Lord, He sees right the way through. I tell myself that long before we were born—from a "human" point of view—Jesus met us somewhere, in Bethlehem, or perhaps Nazareth, or along the road to Galilee—anywhere. And one day among all the other days, his eyes happened to rest upon you and me and so we were called, each in his own particular way, according to the time, place and circumstance.

The young country curé then continues in his diary:

> I hadn't realized there were tears on my face, I wasn't even thinking of it. "What are you blub-

bering for?" The truth is that *my* place for all time has been Mount Olivet; yes, in that instant—strangely in that very instant, when he set his hand on Peter's shoulder asking him the useless question, almost naïve yet so tender, so deeply courteous: *Why sleep ye?* It was a very ordinary, natural reaction of which till then I had been unaware. And suddenly—"What's up now?" The Curé de Torcy snapped again, irritably, "You're not even listening to me. . . ."

I opened my mouth. I meant to answer, but couldn't. Never mind. Isn't it enough that our Lord this day should have granted me, through the lips of my old teacher, the Revelation that I am never to be torn from that eternal place chosen for me—that I remain the prisoner of his Agony in the Garden. Who would dare take such an honor upon himself?[1]

If we were to meet a man like this country priest, we would surely be filled with respect, compassion and perhaps even fear. For he shifts a little of his insupportable burden onto our spirit. But perhaps we will also ask ourselves spontaneously what was the moment in the life of Jesus that determined our vocation? What was the moment in which he looked and touched each one of us individually?

---

[1] Georges Bernanos, *Journal d'un curé de campagne* (1936). English translation: *The Diary of a Country Priest* (New York: Doubleday, Image Books, 1954), 158–59.

If we were to do so, then the expression "the grace of vocation" would reacquire for us all its depth and meaningfulness. We would penetrate into its source in the Gospel and in the life of Jesus himself. We would connect the spiritual gift of our vocation with the spirit of the Lord, and our specific service in the Church with the Lord of the Church. Every vocation, to be sure, has a tangible, objective component of its own. For service necessarily has a concrete end: it always involves a concrete task, and intervenes in the life and action of the Church, materially contributing to her change or her building up. Yet vocation is always more than this. Otherwise it would be synonymous with a worldly orientation; it would become confused with the philosophy of the pleasant life or of action in the "fifth column"; with the pathos of the great objectors who simply say "No thanks!" to everything and everyone; or with the unconditional pacifism of the peace movement.

No, vocation is more than that. Vocation and charism maintain a bond with Jesus Christ himself, from whom they derive their origin. His person is reflected in them. The spiritual mission has the character of a bond in which trust, hope and the support of the Lord are indissolubly merged. Vocation is therefore always the chance given to us of entering into a communion of faith and experience with the Lord.

2. The Many Images of Saint Francis

The memory of Saint Francis of Assisi is one that thousands of people find moving. He is rightly considered one of the great saints in the history of the Faith. Even though we are separated from him by more than eight hundred years of history, his life and work continue to fascinate the men and women of our time.

Admittedly, if we look at the matter a little more closely, we may gain the impression that this fascination with the saint has been turned into an article of fashion, a vogue disseminated by the most varied individuals and groups. And as is always the case, the variety of the image of him thus disseminated does not help its clarity. Here too inflation has the effect of devaluation. The saint is presented to us shimmering with every color in the rainbow.

Saint Francis has lent himself to the most diverse interpretations. The Marxist study of the Middle Ages interprets him according to sociological criteria. On this view, Francis is the precursor of an anticapitalist spirit propagating a propertyless society. Francis, the Marxists say, embodied the dawning consciousness of a new proletarian ideal that vindicated the values of the material world in opposition to the otherwordliness of the Middle Ages.

Another view is that propagated by the proponents of the Romantic interpretation of the saint in the nineteenth century; they admired Francis as a kind of precursor of Rousseau and his theme of "back to nature!" He is presented as the ever blithe and carefree lover of nature, who loved the creation and had no problems in his relationship with the created world. One of these Romantic interpreters, A. Holl, in his book on Francis, even goes so far as to affirm that Francis and Clare were lovers. And in an interview on Vatican Radio, this question posed at the end of the program: "Can one perhaps say that Francis was one of the first hippies?" brought from the priest being interviewed the reply: "Yes, he can really be called that."

Yet another view of Francis is that propagated by critics inside the Church, who recognize in him the saint who above all proclaimed the idea of brotherhood in opposition to the power of the ministry in the Church. In inculcating the need for poverty and in speaking out in favor of the lack of possessions, Francis, it is said, reacted against the feudal structure of the Church; this was his real purpose. His movement thus became an anti-model: an alternative to the imperial structures that had alienated, and still alienate, the Church from the Gospel.

Others again see in him the prototype, the forerunner, of the protector of the environment: the "ecological" saint. Still others (notably under the influence of the spirituality of the Oriental churches) uphold him as the ideal of contemplation, the mystic who really wanted to withdraw from the world.

It is quite possible that a little of all these interpretations is actually to be found in the life of this great man. We cannot but be grateful to him for offering us such a broad range of possible interpretations; for this very many-sidedness makes it easy for us to be convinced of his greatness. On the other hand, we run the risk of totally misunderstanding him by seeing him in this way: we may be tempted, in other words, to subordinate him to our own purposes, to use him simply as a convenient rubber stamp for endorsing our own ideas. But if we misappropriate him in this way, we shall never be able to fathom, still less to elucidate, his mystery. We would confuse the cause with the effect, as if we were to see the wind itself in the rustling of the leaves on the tree.

If we want to come closer to the saint, we can surely be helped to do so by listening to what he himself has to say when he himself expresses himself in words, as for instance in his prayer before the crucifix in the church of San Damiano.

Saint Francis, in the year 1206, was praying inside this almost completely ruined church in the environs of Assisi when he heard the words issuing from the painted image of Christ on the Cross:

"Francis, go, repair my house, which, as you see, is falling completely to ruin." Thomas of Celano, in his "Second Life of the Saint", adds the following comment:

> Trembling, Francis was not a little amazed and became almost deranged by these words. He prepared himself to obey and gave himself completely to the fulfillment of this command. But since he felt that the change he had undergone was beyond expression, it is becoming that we should be silent about what he could not express.

His willingness to serve the as yet unspecified mission of the Lord was total; he offered himself totally and without reservation to the will of God. Important in this regard is Thomas of Celano's further comment: "From then on compassion for the crucified was rooted in his holy soul."[2] Hereafter, a condition for the fulfillment of a task given to us by God is compassion for and recognition of Christ crucified. In other words, true wisdom is the "wisdom of the Cross". This alone ensures a reliable orientation in approaching the question as to God's will and mission.

In the hour of this meeting with the Lord, this great saint formulated the following prayer, which epitomizes his confession of faith:

[2] Marion A. Habig, ed., *St. Francis of Assisi, Writings and Early Biographies. English Omnibus of the Sources for the Life of St. Francis* (Chicago: Franciscan Herald Press, 1983), 370.

Almighty and glorious God,
lighten the darkness of my heart
and give me true faith,
steadfast hope and perfect love.
Give me, Lord,
[true] feeling and knowledge,
so that I may accomplish your holy task
which you have given me in truth. Amen.[3]

This meeting of Saint Francis with the crucified Lord was developed during his whole life in many facets. It stresses features in our picture of the "Poverello" that elude the caprice of modern interpretation. Yet they are inseparably bound up with the development of his divine mission and of enduring value. Moreover, they are so closely bound up with the mystery of Christ himself that they experience an astonishing rebirth in other witnesses of the Faith.

They do so in another geat man who lived seven hundred years later, a man, that is, of our time. He turned his whole life into a mission that made many of his contemporaries sit up and take notice. I refer to the French scholar and monk Charles de Foucauld. That he was familiar with the long-famous man from Assisi is certain. Yet the voluminous writings of Charles de Foucauld provide no evidence that he had in any special way concerned himself with this saint. Despite this lack of

[3] K. Esser, ed., *Die Schriften des Hl. Franz von Assisi* (Werl/ Westphalia, 1962), 166.

explicit evidence, his spiritual impulses, as well as some similarities detectable in the course of his life, betray a surprising degree of affinity with those of Francis.

3. Selfless Dedication to His Fellowmen

Brother Charles of Jesus, as Charles de Foucauld (1859–1916) called himself after his conversion, came to understand ever more clearly in the course of his life that he had been called to become a "brother to all men". God transformed him from a roué and pleasure-seeker first into a distinguished ethnographer and linguist and then into a Trappist monk and domestic in Nazareth, before finally leading him into the Sahara, into the heartland of the Tuareg, a nomadic tribe, to whom he tried to be a brother.

During a spiritual retreat before Christmas in 1904, he wrote:

How to practice equality and brotherhood with the natives? Answer: by letting them approach me ever more closely, and letting them speak with me . . . without fear of sacrificing my time to them. . . . Instead of running away from their long speeches, let me wish that they come to me, but always directing them to God; taking the lead in such conversations in order to turn them away from the earth and direct them to spiritual things. To have no fear of contact with the natives, with their clothes and blankets, etc. . . . To have no fear of their filth, their stench. . . . Above all, to see Jesus in them and therefore to treat them not just as equals and brothers, but with the humility, respect, love and veneration that such a faith demands.

And in another passage of his journals he writes:

Strive to enter into spiritual communion whenever I enter the chapel, whenever I speak with someone, whenever I write to someone.[4]

What this means in practice is spelled out for us in a letter of August 29, 1902:

I wish for myself, and consequently wish also for you, a little solitude and silence, because I consider them very good. On the one hand, I feel very alone here, because I have not even one person here who is in the least degree attached to me. . . . On the other hand, I am speaking with and listening to people without interruption from half past four in the morning to half past eight in the evening. Slaves, poor people, invalids, soldiers, travelers and the curious. . . .

To give you some inkling of what my life is really like, you must know that people knock at my

---

[4] D. Barrat, ed., *Oeuvres spirituels de Charles de Foucauld* (Paris, 1958), 568f.

door at least ten times every hour—poor people, sick people, passers-by; so that I have not only a great deal of quiet, but also a great deal of bustle.[5]

In all this, Charles de Foucauld displayed exemplary dedication to his fellowmen. But this was never mere philanthropy, never a mere humanism that simply wants to do good to other people. For if ever a person has testified, in a manner too striking to be ignored, that dedication to our fellowmen is prompted by the search for the Lord in our neighbor and directed at the Lord himself, that person was Brother Charles de Foucauld. On almost every page of his numerous meditations on love for our neighbor he repeats that what we do to our neighbor, we do to the Lord himself. In him there is no trace of the complicated reflection that we should not seek man for the love of God but should accept him for his own sake. We do not find in him the erroneous exegesis of the parable of judgment (cf. Mt 25:31ff.: "I say to you, as you did it to one of the least of these my brethren, you did it to me"), which asserts that the benefactors of mankind will recognize Jesus himself in the needy only at the time of the Last Judgment, and which thus draws the conclusion that if the faithful do good to their fellowmen they should do so not for the love of Jesus but for man's own sake.

[5] Ibid., 708.

4. Signposts of a Lover on the Way to Christ

The best prayer is the one that contains the most
  love.

Rejoice in the fact that God is simply God.

If one loves, one wants above all else to be together.

Symbol of a love eternally young (his vow of
  celibacy).

Worship, this silent adoration that contains the
  most passionate declarations of love.

These sentences of Charles de Foucauld speak
for themselves. The Abbé Huvelin, his spiritual
director and confessor, said of him: "He is capable
of making a love story out of religion." A further
passage from his writings is exemplary:

Welcoming our neighbor means welcoming a
member of Jesus, a part of his body, a member of
Jesus himself; everything we say or do to our
neighbor is consequently heard and experienced
by Jesus: it is to him that we say it, it is to him that
we do it.[6]

The selfless dedication to his fellowmen, which
so arouses our admiration for Brother Charles,
also distinguished the life of Francis of Assisi. His
discovery of Jesus in his suffering fellow human
beings was full of consequence, as is generally well
known. It is especially his first biographer, Thom-

[6] Ibid., 188.

as of Celano, who brings his home to us. Lepers, he tells us, had always filled Francis with feelings of disgust and abhorrence. He could not tolerate the sight of their putrifying limbs, still less the stench they emanated. He therefore tried to avoid them, and whenever he happened to bump into them, he would make a wide detour, holding his nose. Then one day, riding near Assisi, he happened to meet a man afflicted with this "scourge of mankind". Naturally, feelings of revulsion and horror were once again aroused in Francis. But he succeeded in mastering them and got off his horse. He had the feeling that "the Lord himself had led him there". First, he gave the outcast what money he had with him. Then, overcoming his repugnance, he embraced the leper and kissed him.

In the days that followed, Francis repeated this gesture of affection to other lepers: "He went to the dwelling places of the lepers, and after he had given each leper some money, he kissed his hand and his mouth."[7] Thus, Francis too discovered Christ in his fellowmen, and he did so in just those suffering from the most loathsome diseases. He called them "our Christian brothers".[8] How strongly this experience marked the life of Saint Francis is shown, for instance, by another episode. One day a brother expressed a harsh judgment about a poor man. Francis rebuked him and said:

[7] Habig, op. cit., 369–70.
[8] Ibid., 998.

When you see a poor man, you must see in him
the one in whose name he comes, namely, Christ,
who took our poverty and frailty upon himself.
For the frailty and poverty of that man are for us a
mirror in which, full of compassion, we should
see the frailty and poverty of our Lord Jesus Christ
which he bore on his body for our salvation.[9]

Those who adopt as their own Jesus' teaching
about the least of our brethren and embody it in
their lives with such exemplary selflessness as
Francis of Assisi and Charles de Foucauld may ir-
ritate us. Faced by them, we may be prompted to
justify ourselves and speak glibly of inhuman or at
least unreasonable conduct. But instead of making
such pleas, it would surely be more honorable if
we were simply to recognize our fear, admit our
egoism and then ask God for greater love through
the intercession of Saint Francis.

5. Deep Personal Attachment to the God-Man, Jesus of Nazareth

Charles de Foucauld underwent his conversion
in Paris in late October 1880. He later wrote to H.
de Castries about his experience:

---

[9] Francis of Assisi, in P. Manns, ed., *Die Heiligen in ihrer
Zeit*, vol. 2 (Mainz, 1966), 86f. Cf. Thomas of Celano in
Habig, op. cit., 293.

As soon as I believed that a God exists I recognized that I could only live for him. Ever since the moment of my conversion I have been conscious of my vocation to live for God alone. [10]

Under the guidance of his spiritual director, the Abbé Huvelin, de Foucauld's unconditional willingness to serve the Lord became increasingly transformed into a deep and quite human attachment to Jesus of Nazareth. This was expressed at first in the efforts made by Brother Charles to imitate the life of Jesus of Nazareth with total dedication and absolute fidelity. He became a Trappist monk in the French monastery of Notre Dame des Neiges. A year later he confessed to his friend Henri Duveyer:

Why did I join the Trappists? . . . Out of love. . . . I love our Lord Jesus Christ. I do so with a heart that would like to love him more and better; but in any case I love him and cannot bear leading any other life than his own. How can I live an agreeable and honorable life, if his was the harshest and most unrecognized ever? [11]

After a period spent in the monastery, he wrote to his spiritual director on September 2, 1893, to explain why he found it necessary to leave the Trappists. He did not want to cut himself off from

[10] J.-F. Six, *Itinéraire spirituelle de Charles de Foucauld* (Paris, 1959), 58.

[11] Letter of April 24, 1890.

the life of humility, from the insignificant life of Nazareth that he had always sought. He wanted to lead this life together with Jesus, and share the joy of the Mother of God and Saint Joseph in Jesus' love and for the sake of Jesus' love.

After several years of patient waiting, in 1896 he was eventually given permission by his spiritual director to go to Nazareth and live in the very place where Jesus himself had lived. Charles de Foucauld set out on his journey, his fascination with the person of Jesus only strengthened. Consumed with boundless curiosity, he set about gathering all the possible information about Jesus he could find and making it his own. In a passage of the meditations with which he filled thousands of pages of notebooks at Nazareth, he observed:

> Small and humble, I undertake the reading of the Bible with the wish to read it through from beginning to end, my gaze fixed on God alone, so that I may get to know him better, to love him and serve him. As a poor servant in Nazareth, I usually read before the holy tabernacle, at the end of the day, when the work is finished and night begins to fall.[12]

In another passage (1902) he notes:

> We must try to imbue ourselves with the spirit of Jesus by reading and meditating again and again on his word and example; they must be for us like

[12] Barrat, op. cit., 69.

the drop of water which falls again and again on
the same spot on the stone.

This close attachment to the person of Jesus
Christ explains the rare profundity of the veneration that Brother Charles devoted to the eucharistic Lord. At Nazareth he spent up to eight hours a
day meditating on the Gospel before the taberna-
cle. It is told that on the day after his arrival in the
hometown of Jesus, he went to the convent of the
Poor Clares even before daybreak to pray before
the Holy Sacrament. When the bell rang for the
midday repast at eleven o'clock, Brother Charles
signaled to the lay sister in charge of the kitchen to
go away. The sister did not dare to contradict him
but kept an eye on Brother Charles through the
chapel window. She could not imagine how anyone could pray for so long and feared that this
stranger in their midst was actually intent on steal-
ing the monstrance!

Brother Charles himself describes his eucharistic prayer:

> Because you are always with us in the Holy Eu-
> charist, we want to be with you always; we want
> to share your company before the tabernacle; we
> don't want to lose even one moment which we
> could have spent before it through our own fault.
> God is there: Why should we go and seek some-
> thing else? Our Loved One, our All is there. He
> invites us to be at his side—and do we not hasten
> to do so? Would we spend elsewhere even a single

moment of the time we could spend at his side? Everything else—pictures, relics, pilgrimages, books—is all very well, and God allows this or that person to make use of these things as a means of finding their way to him, so that they may be guided by him and come to love and get to know him better. But all these means are inanimate objects. We want to make use of them if Jesus commands us to do so, if he makes it known to us that this is his will. But as far as we are concerned, it is to the Eucharist, and nowhere else, that we want to go. The Holy Eucharist is Jesus, it is the Lord in his entirety![13]

Such declarations may give the impression that Charles de Foucauld was a sentimental egoist in search of feelings of piety for their own sake. But we would be quite mistaken to believe so. For his love was not just sentimental: it gave birth to the action that proves its authenticity. It was through his love for Jesus that he penetrated ever more deeply into the spirit of the imitation of Christ. He wanted to be as close to Christ as it was possible tobe. He wanted to be like the Lord. Not of course the Lord in his greatness, his miracles and his powerful preaching, but the poor and humiliated Lord, the despised and rejected Jesus—this he took as his model.

Charles de Foucauld was convinced that self-renunciation and self-sacrifice are the most con-

[13] Ibid., 790.

vincing proofs of true love. He therefore strove to identify himself with the Lord by sharing a similar life of poverty. Let us listen again to his own words:

> My Lord Jesus, how speedily will the person who cannot bear to be richer than you, because he loves you with all his heart, become poor! . . . I don't know how it is possible for some people to see you poor and yet gladly remain rich and so see themselves so much greater than you, their master, their beloved Lord; how it is possible for them not to be like you in everything. . . . I would so much like them to love you, my God, but I believe something is lacking in their love; in any case, I cannot conceive of love without the need, without the compelling need, for conformity, for similarity [with the loved one] and especially for participation in all the sufferings, all the difficulties, all the tribulations of life. [14]

6. Poverty in Imitation of Christ

Whoever testifies to these words with the witness of his own life cannot leave us indifferent. We adopt a stance. We may place the case of Charles de Foucauld among the eccentrics and odd-men-out of history and be too quick to reject him.

[14] Ibid., 520.

Or we may become troubled in our conscience and feel that the demands placed on us by such a life are too great. But perhaps we may also be attracted by so much heroism and dream ourselves of self-renunciation, self-humbling and sacrifice. But what if Brother Charles with his embodiment of the Gospel of Jesus were to be transformed for us into a thorn in our flesh? For the Lord's demand for poverty is one we all too gladly suppress in our affluent society. And, besides, who actually likes to be humiliated?

Nonetheless, poverty and humility are inseparable from Jesus and his message, a message that Brother Charles transformed for us into a living testimony to the Gospel and the person of Jesus Christ.

The key word, *poverty*, immediately reminds us of Francis of Assisi. His actions, his words and his writings are a standing admonishment to poverty. Thus, his last will for the sisters of Saint Clare, consisting of only three sentences, recalls this evangelical counsel no less than twice. He speaks of his wish to embrace a life of poverty and then urges the sisters to do likewise:

> I, little Brother Francis, wish to live according to the life and poverty of our most high Lord Jesus Christ and his most holy Mother and to persevere in this to the last. And I beseech you, my ladies, and I exhort you to live always in this most holy life and poverty. Keep close watch over your-

selves so that you never abandon it through the teaching or advice of anyone.[15]

He often called poverty "my Lady". He also linked poverty with the concept of humility, as for example in his *Praises of the Virtues*: "Lady Holy Poverty, God keep you, with your sister, holy Humility."[16] In this way, he preserved the idea of poverty from being misconstrued as superficiality or as a merely literal and formal practice.

A careful reading of the writings of Saint Francis helps us, moreover, to guard against a number of misinterpretations of poverty. Modern concepts of poverty, which are the product of political or ideological systems or which place emphasis on the social and economic aspects, cannot in any way help to clarify what Francis meant by the term. More particularly, they leave out of account his point of departure, which is always bound up with the person of Christ. This becomes clear, for instance, when we examine more closely his use of the expression "following in the footsteps of Christ". This is another key element of his spirituality that profoundly linked the whole of his thought with the Gospel. It linked the attitude and action of Francis with the person of Jesus himself, and constitutes another common feature shared by Charles de Foucauld and Francis of Assisi.

[15] Habig, op. cit., 76.
[16] Ibid., 132.

For me, however, more surprising than this affinity was the recognition that a significant parallelism also existed between these two great men of the Church in their evaluation of the Eucharist. In the writings of the "Poverello", the Sacrament of the Body of Jesus occupies a conspicuous position. Again and again he recurs to the mystery of the Eucharist, and he bequeathed numerous instructions and exhortations relating to it to posterity. It is a theme that occupies a privileged place in his writings, especially in his *Admonitions*, his *Letter to a General Chapter*, his *Letter to All Superiors of the Friars Minor*, his *Letter to All the Faithful* and his *Letter to All Clerics*: all these writings show the great importance that Francis of Assisi attached to the sacrament of the Eucharist.[17]

This veneration for the Body and Blood of Christ is accompanied, as in Brother Charles of Jesus, by respect for the Word of God. This is shown not only by the many quotations from the Gospels to be found in the writings of Saint Francis (though this in itself was unusual in the thirteenth century) but also by his repeated exhortation of the need to respect the written Word of God; this entailed the obligation to collect together all copies of the Bible and keep them in a fitting place. Yet the most striking proof of Francis' veneration for Holy Scripture is his repeated

[17] Ibid., 91–113 passim.

call that we take the Word of God as the norm for
our action: "Live according to the Holy Gospel."
In his *Testament*, Francis writes: "The Most High
himself made it clear to me that I must live the life
of the Gospel."[18]

It is beyond the scope of this study to pursue
any further these affinities between the lives of
Charles de Foucauld and Francis of Assisi. Yet a
summary comparison has shown an impressive
degree of unanimity between them in their evaluation of the Word of God, the Eucharist and poverty in humility. It would be possible to point out
other key points in their system of spiritual coordinates, such as the value both men attached to
obedience, or their loving veneration of Mary,
who occupies a preeminent place in the prayers of
both and with whom both repeatedly sought spiritual communion.

7. The Saints as the Way to Christ

More significant than these affinities in spirituality is the fact that these fixed points in their system of spiritual coordinates do not only make
sense in themselves; more important, they were
discovered and stressed by both men because they
are particularly reliable factors for personal union

[18] Ibid., 68.

with Jesus Christ, bridges for a personal communion with the Lord.

Biographies of Saint Francis have pointed out the stages through which the Saint of Assisi grew to an ever greater identification, an ever more intimate union, with Jesus Christ. For my present purposes, I can touch on these only briefly.

All began with the vision of Christ that Francis had before the crucifix in the ruined little church of San Damiano. So overpowing was this vision that it moved the saint to extraordinarily heightened spiritual experiences. He began to tremble and was struck dumb by astonishment. His first biographer, Thomas of Celano, describes the effect of this meeting with Christ:

> From that hour on, his soul was melted when his Beloved spoke to him . . . and from then on he could never keep himself from weeping, even bewailing in a loud voice the Passion of Christ which was always, as it were, before his mind.[19]

Through this vision, Christ entered physically into the life of Saint Francis. It transformed him to such an extent that his life was henceforth to be understood exclusively in relation to that of Jesus. His life was henceforth modeled entirely on that of Jesus Christ, and in so exclusive a way that it is hardly paralleled in the life of any other believer.

[19] Ibid., 371.

Jesus completely transformed the life of Saint Francis.

In following in the footsteps of Christ, Francis not only discovered the Lord glorified in heaven. More than his contemporaries, he turned to the Gospel as the source that told of the *earthly* life of Jesus. Thus, not only the Lord transfigured, but also the Lord humiliated, became for him essential: the whole life of Jesus, from his birth in Bethlehem onward, stood at the very centerpoint of his devotion. Francis, both in his life and in his teaching, made the Faith tangible: he turned it into something that could be embodied and experienced. He retrieved the meaning of the events of Jesus' life from the mists of history and brought it back into full daylight once again. Jesus could once again be accepted by ordinary people as a man and a brother.

Here no doubt lies a central point of the importance of Saint Francis for the history of devotion in the Church and for the pilgrimage of faith of us all. Both cannot but acquire renewed vigor from Francis' achievement in making the events of the Gospel and the earthly life of Jesus accessible to us. And this brings us back, by a lengthy detour, to the affirmations of the writer Georges Bernanos quoted at the beginning of this chapter.

Yet in the case of Francis of Assisi the bond with Christ leads even further: it is as if, in the life of the "Poverello", Jesus were once again to become visible to man. Walter Nigg, a well-known biographer of saints in our time, writes in this regard:

> This is what is ineffable, what one cannot find appropriate words to express, because whatever one might say sounds so inadequate and does not convey any true idea of this ardent fire. For Francis, Jesus was not a thing of the past, but a living reality that haunted him night and day. . . . Francis found himself in a mystic closeness to Jesus which wiped out all historical distance between them. The Jesus of the Gospel once again took shape in him, and in so compelling a way that it is hardly equaled either before or after.[20]

By contemplating the figure of Saint Francis, we thus find it easier—easier than with almost any other great figure of the Church—to imbue all study of the lives of the saints with its deepest meaning. The essence of this deepest meaning is explained to us by Brother Charles of Jesus, who once said about veneration of the saints:

> Let us contemplate the saints. Yet let us not linger in contemplating them. Let us rather contemplate with them the One whose contemplation filled their lives! Let us make use of their example, but without dwelling too long on it, without choosing this or that saint as our only model. Let us take from each what seems to us to correspond best to the word and example of our Lord Jesus; for he is

[20] W. Nigg, *Grosse Heilige* (Zurich, 1958), 49f.

our only true model. In this way we shall make
use of their teachings, not to imitate *them*, but the
better to be able to imitate Jesus. [21]

These reflections may perhaps give the impression of lacking any reference to the group or community. I am quite aware that they are entirely
focused on the individual's gift of grace: that spiritual movements, communities and associations
are here excluded from the picture. In spite of this,
I believe that these reflections can also prove fruit-
ful and rewarding for communities and groups.
For my chosen perspective here, the focus on the
individual (in this case the saint) is in no way intended to deny or place in question the meaningfulness of Church groups with spiritual and
apostolic objectives. Such a denial could be especially misplaced in the case of Francis of Assisi and
Charles de Foucauld, both of whom are eloquent
examples of the value of associations and communities for the life of the Church and the spreading
of the Gospel.

Reflection on our own times shows, indeed,
that association not only has a sense, but is indispensable for those who want to survive. Leading
psychologists say this about the chances for sur-
vival of the individual today: alone, the individual
hasn't a hope. Oppressed by a system of government that dominates his whole life, manipulated

---

[21] Barrat, op. cit., 13.

and intimidated by a series of overpowering stimuli, the individual cannot cope alone; he thus has a need for a group that, alongside the family, can transmit values and aspirations and overcome his own frailty and contradictions.

In spite of this indispensable role played by the group, the role of the individual must not be overlooked or minimized, also in the field of spiritual life. The individual always stands in a dialectical tension between himself and the group as a whole. This tension between the individual and the community must not be eliminated at the expense of either: the actions of both are mutually interdependent.

Especially in the history of salvation, the individual cannot hide behind the community. For it is in the individual that redemption occurs and through the individual, in the imitation of Christ, that redemption is achieved. That such distinctive figures in the history of Christianity as Francis of Assisi and Charles de Foucauld could in the long term become the founders of vital and enduring religious communities is inseparably bound up with this: they both underwent, in their different ways, a radical conversion, that is, they returned to God and were thus able to live an original and convincing expression of the Christian life.

III

EXPERIENCE AS AN AID TO FAITH: CHRISTIAN WITNESS IN CULTURE, THE FAMILY AND THE WORLD OF WORK

Psychologists and sociologists have convincingly shown that human life corresponds with the environment in which it is lived. It is man's environment, his *Lebensraum*, that determines the impressions made on him. "Milieu" constitutes the lasting source of his knowledge, the lasting educator of his will. This constant influence is especially apparent in man's meeting with culture, in his relationships within the family and in his coming to terms with the demands of the world of work. These three spheres of human activity do not of course exhaust the range of the human environment. Yet it is here that the essential sectors of the milieu in which man lives are most tangible, most immediately penetrate and have an effect on him.

In the discussion that follows, the fields of experience offered by culture, the family and the world of work shall be considered from a theological perspective. These three dimensions of human existence are, thanks to their power for molding character, especially suitable for the transmission of the Gospel. Whoever wants to be apostolically active is thus faced with the task of giving a Christian formation to these three spheres of life.

Culture, the family and the world of work also form the three particular areas in which laypersons exercise their characteristic vocation to apostolic activity. The lay apostolate, like any other form of proclaiming the Gospel, can be understood as a form of commitment aimed at making the Faith experienceable. Through such lay involvement the fabric of social life can be transformed, Christian signposts raised and the Gospel bring meaning in a new way. Yet in involving themselves in society, Christians are continually confronted by the manifold difficulties of relating faith and life.

Here, it is the task of theologians to examine how the teachings of the Faith can be translated into human experience, to elucidate the interrelationships between the two and to ascertain the degree to which the content of the Faith can actually be derived from experience.

A study written by Edward Schillebeeckx in 1979 seems a useful starting point for an investigation of this kind, since it examines the relationship between faith and experience. The book contains the following key ideas: people at times experience fundamental, overwhelming and profoundly moving personal events, events that push back the borders of their past experience, both of their individual lives and of the world itself. The person who experiences such an event cannot classify it in a routine fashion. Its meaning remains ambiguous to him. At times it may be possible to relate such extraordinary experiences to Jesus Christ or God. When a Christian attempts to interpret a profound experience in this way, he may find that some truth of the Faith is directly revealed to him. In a flash he may suddenly recognize its truth: "Yes," he says to himself, "that's how it is; that's it!"

Through such experiences man is confronted with the Gospel's redeeming power and is enabled to see how God liberates him through his work of salvation. What had hitherto merely been thought of or known about through the proclamation of the Word as a possibility of the Christian life (Schillebeeckx calls this the *Suchprojekt*, the Christian's search for God as a result of the Gospel proclamation) is transformed by such experiences into "a wholly personal act of faith, a personal conviction of faith with a concrete content of Christian faith".[1] According to Schillebeeckx, it is in this way that man today accepts the credo of the Christian faith: the Christian faith proceeds from the

---

[1] Edward Schillebeeckx, *Menschliche Erfahrung und Glaube an Jesus Christ: Eine Rechenschaft* (Freiburg, 1979). The book consists of a summation or restatement of the theological conception implicit in the author's two major works: *Jesus: Die Geschichte eines Lebenden* (Freiburg, 1978) and *Christus und die Christen* (Freiburg, 1977).

Christian interpretation of human experience in such a way that experience forms the basis for faith.

This analysis is undoubtedly a very persuasive one for the modern mentality. And no one can doubt its great catechetical effectiveness. According to this interpretation, the certainty of faith is no longer based on the Word or on the conviction of others; faith is something that has to be experienced by believers themselves; it is something that has to exist in their own experience. The content of the Faith passes without mediation into their life experience. Its truth no longer refers to something hereafter, to some special dimension that is perceived as alien or unrelated to everyday life. The truth of Revelation, and hence the power of the Gospel to convince, is rather to be found within the fabric of social life itself.

This interpretation of the close interrelationship between faith and experience is one to which the lay apostolate in particular is only too ready to give its grateful assent. For it is continuously confronted anew with the problem posed by the seeming incompatibility between the truths propounded by the Faith and the realities of the living world. It continuously faces the need to intervene evangelistically in the dimensions of everyday life, in the reality of the creation itself, and this means recognizing, defining and bringing to fruition the spheres in which redemption can take place. It thus seems appropriate to apply the thesis of experience as the basis of faith to the three fields—culture, the family and the world of work—to which my present reflections are addressed.

1. The Experience of Faith and the Christian's Cultural Mission

Here it is not my purpose to postulate concrete forms of apostolate that could be applied to present-day culture, nor to elucidate the inner philosophical and anthropological relationship between culture and the life of man, in the way that the Holy Father so convincingly did during his visits to Paris (1979) and Cologne (1980). For understandable reasons, however, one or two fundamental concepts do need to be explained.

First, what is culture and how does it come into being? In the various spheres of their personal and social lives, people fashion and invent forms to order life or to make it more pleasant; these include everything from housing and clothing to science and religion. These forms of expression are at the same time the means by which man emerges from his anonymity and gives himself a recognizable identity.

It is especially through language, myth and art that man interprets himself and his history. With the help of culture, man succeeds in understanding himself better. He finds himself reflected in culture and gives himself objective expression in it. Through culture, man gains a more accurate idea of what he is and how he should judge himself.

A sense of community spirit develops hand in hand with this sense of cultural identity and historical self-awareness. If religious elements or recognizably Christian human values also form part of this community spirit, then a society has the duty to express them in symbolic terms, along with every other aspect of its culture. If it failed to do so, the religious dimension of man's spiritual world would be weakened or reduced because the symbolic world that had been created would be inadequate. It would no longer be a faithful image of the real-life world.

At the same time, the lack of adequate religious expression in that society's culture would mean that a great pastoral opportunity would have been lost. This opportunity must be examined and taken into account, even though due care must be taken not to destroy culture by instrumentalizing it. It springs from the fact that religious culture forms man and that a wide range of symbols may be extremely effective as signs proclaiming the Word. The process of creating cultural objects attains its end only when these objects are understood and appropriated in themselves; in other words, when those who observe them, and those to whom they are addressed, accept the signs and

give their assent to the values that the signs represent. Christian culture—certainly as grace and
channel for grace—works in this way, since it em-
bodies a message and proclaims it both to individuals and to the community.

The conversion of the French poet Paul Claudel
may help to explain the point. As is well known,
Claudel lost his faith in his youth and in adult life
succumbed to "a state of despair". At the same
time he felt a great spiritual hunger inside him.
More out of curiosity than devotion, he happened
to enter Notre Dame Cathedral in Paris on Christmas Day 1886. He attended the Solemn High
Mass, as he recalled, "with a mild degree of plea-
sure" and later returned to the cathedral for vespers. He subsequently described in detail what he
saw of the Divine Office and the place where he
was standing in the cathedral:

> The choirboys were singing what I later discov-
> ered to be the "Magnificat". I was standing in the
> crowd, near the second pillar at the entrance to the
> choir on the right, by the sacristy. And it was then
> that the event took place that changed my whole
> life. In an instant, my heart was touched, and I
> believed. [2]

[2] "Les enfants de la maîtrise . . . étaient en train de chanter
ce que je sus plus tard être le Magnificat. J'étais moi-même de-
bout du second pilier, à l'entrée du choeur à droite du côté de
la sacristie. Et c'est alors que ce produisit l'événement qui domini toute ma vie. En un instant mon coeur fut touché et je

To be sure, an event of this kind cannot be plumbed in its depths. Not even the person who experiences it is able to provide a cogent explanation of it, for the process by which man gives himself to God is a mystery. Yet while as a whole it remains ineffable, several contributory factors can be grasped. First, the feast itself must have been important for Claudel, as also the community at prayer in which he found himself. Second, the liturgy of the Mass, as the specific form of prayer the Church has created through the centuries as the expression of her faith and her esthetic sense, must also have played a significant role in Claudel's experience. Third, the place itself, the milieu in which it took place, must also have had a particular influence on the event: a Gothic cathedral of overpowering beauty in which the artistic sense of generations and the will to adore God have been given formal expression in stone. (It is no coincidence that Claudel mentions three times the exact place in the cathedral in which his conversion took place.) We all know the influence that such a place can have on our state of mind: the way man is made to feel so small and yet so uplifted, the way it opens his heart and makes him receptive to the world of the Spirit.

---

crus." Quoted in A. Lagarde and L. Michard, eds, *Texte et littérature, XXème siècle* (Paris, 1962), 177.

Paul Claudel's experience of conversion bears witness to the faith-giving power of a culture created by faith. An interplay of many elements was at work when he entered the cathedral and attended the Divine Office being celebrated in it: the music, the chant and the language, the sacred enactment of the liturgy, those by whom it was performed and officiated, their movements, vestments and rites, the community itself whose interior participation he was able to sense and the whole architectural setting, with its combination of color, light and shadow.

How profoundly this experience must have revealed to Claudel the great value that the celebration of the Divine Office in the house of God has for believers! Whoever has been vouchsafed such an experience can surely understand the lament uttered by the man in the Old Testament praying from his place of exile so far from Jerusalem:

As the doe longs for running streams,
so longs my soul for you, my God.

My soul thirsts for God, the God of life;
when shall I go and see the face of God?

I have no food but tears, day and night;
and all day long men say to me, "Where is your God?"

I remember, and my soul melts within me;
I am on my way to the wonderful Tent, to the house of
   God,

among cries of joy and praise and an exultant throng.
                                                      — Psalm 42:1–5

Or with the Psalmist who says:

O Lord, I love the house where you live,
the place where your glory makes its home.
                                                      — Psalm 26:8

What God is able to reveal through his temple of his joyful presence and the greatness of his majesty was suddenly made clear to Claudel on that Christmas Day in 1886. In an instant, in a flash, the truth was revealed to him: "Yes, that's how it is; that's it."

At this point one ought to quote at length from the Old Testament to show how Claudel's experience placed him in the company of so many others who have shared the same experience: Isaiah, Micah, Zechariah, Ezekiel. This chain of prophets reaches right through to the New Testament, to the words and deeds of Jesus Christ himself, who practiced his devotions in the temple that was his Father's house (cf. Lk 2:41ff.) and who protested against the profanation of the temple in Jerusalem (Mk 11:15–19).

Anyone who appreciates the power of God's temple to enkindle and fan the fire of faith, anyone who has experienced the house of God as Revelation, will find it hard to understand why this appears to be called into question in the final books of the New Testament. Does not Jesus appear to deny all the values the temple symbolized when, in the Gospel of Saint John, he tells the woman of Samaria: "Woman, believe me, the hour is coming when neither on this mountain nor in Jerusalem will you worship the Father. . . . But the hour is coming, and now is, when the true worshippers will worship the Father in spirit and truth, for such the Father seeks to worship him. God is spirit, and those who worship him must worship in spirit and truth" (Jn 4:21–24); or when the author of Revelation says of the heavenly Jerusalem: "And I saw no temple in the city, for its temple is the Lord God the Almighty and the Lamb" (Rev 21:22).

We cannot here go into the question why these biblical statements do not preclude a new Christian form of worship, with its own liturgy. What more particularly concerns us at the moment is the significance of the experience granted in the act of faith. And in evaluating the value of personal experience as the basis for a man's faith, we are bound to declare that the apparent denial of the house of God and temple worship implied by the passages from Saint John's Gospel and Revelation quoted above is not something we can spontaneously accept. Our own experience flies in the face of it. We are unable to reconcile the liberating power by which God saves us with the destruction of the house of God and the suppression of the liturgy. Anyone deprived of these sources of support for the strengthening of his faith cannot but be reminded of the words of the faithful in the Old Testament who "by the waters in Babylon . . . sat down and wept", and found themselves unable to sing the Lord's song in a foreign land, far from the temple in Jerusalem (cf. Ps 137).

In the light of these reflections and Jesus' teaching that God be worshipped in the Spirit, the first doubts emerge about the accuracy of the thesis that Edward Schillebeeckx supports with such absolute conviction: namely, that the redeeming power of the fundamental content of the Faith can be made evident through experience. If we were to take this a stage further, the possibilities that culture offers for transmitting the Faith—however legitimate—would be pushed to their extreme limit. For the question then arises whether the means at the disposal of culture are able to promote the transmission of God's Revelation, or whether they might actually be a stumbling block to the propagation of a number of particular truths of the Faith. After all, Jesus taught that God had to be worshipped in the Spirit, and this type of worship not only excludes any created intermediary, but hardly needs any material element, as culture is, to underpin it. A clash thus arises between the claims of "worship in spirit and truth" and "the world of culture": the appeal exerted by culture may even prevent the Spirit of God from revealing himself.

2. Social Commitment

A further aspect of our discussion of experience as an aid to faith concerns the world of work. It should at least be mentioned that important and far-reaching teachings of the Church and of our present Holy Father exist on this theme; indeed, hardly any of the major Church documents in our time fail to touch on it. One of the most significant is John Paul II's papal encyclical *Laborem Exercens* of September 14, 1981.

The purpose of our present investigation is to examine whether it is possible to experience the truths of the Faith in the field of social commitment and how far the data of Revelation are capable of being experienced in it. To this end, the theological aspects of social commitment and service to our fellowmen need to be elucidated. This means that we need to pursue our examination of the questions we raised at the outset: namely, whether it is possible to relate the truths of the Faith (for instance, the New Testament commandment of love for our neighbor) to the Christian's social and political commitment and whether, by being experienced in such commitment, they can become certitudes for us.

No biblical text has made a deeper impression on the modern public conscience, or had such far-reaching consequences, as the words spoken by Jesus: "Truly, I say to you, as you did it to one of the least of these my brethren, you did it to me" (Mt 25:40). Perhaps no other New Testament text has been the subject of such exhaustive discussion as this commandment to practice brotherly love. At all events, this is the impression one gets if one lives in Germany; no doubt the same applies to public opinion in other Western countries. The mass media of all kinds and organizations of whatever ideological origin all show a strong concern for humanitarian action. Even though this does not necessarily mean that brotherly love is actually being practiced, it is a sure sign that there is popular support for the general theory. If one loves one's neighbor, one recognizes and theoretically accepts the implications of this love in the socio-political sphere: the defense of human rights.

There is no doubt that Christians may often experience in their private lives what the New Testament commandment to love one another actually involves. In encountering a needy neighbor or the victims of poverty and destitution, they discover what Jesus meant when he spoke of "the least of these my brethren". Yet if the scope of the new commandment is restricted merely to the sphere of the individual, its biblical sense is likely to be watered down or wrongly understood.

The claims recently made by the so-called liberation theology make any such limitation quite impossible. In support of such claims, mention may be made in the first place of the political and social teachings of the Old Testament writings that speak of the progress and liberation of the chosen people. But in the New Testament, too, brotherly love is not solely concerned with the individual and his duty to love even his enemy, since all people can be our neighbor through Christ (see the parable of the Last Judgment in which the words referring to "the least of these my brethren" occur). More important, this love must be a love not just for individuals but for the whole of humanity: it must be like the loving kindness of God himself (cf. Titus 3:4) and go out to all people (Rom 12:10–12).

Because of this commandment of love, the preaching of Jesus and the New Testament authors often level very sharp criticisms against society, as in their frequently repeated warnings against the rich and the people with established positions in society (cf. Lk 6:24ff.; Mt 6:24; 1 Cor 11:20; James 2:1ff.) and the way they take the side of the poor and the weak (cf. Lk 6:20; 1 Cor 12:22 ff.). That it is not only individuals who are called to change their conscience is implicit in this teaching. Individual righteousness and an orderly life lived in peace and harmony cannot alone remain the goals of private life in society. Christians should also ensure that the new commandment be kept in social structures and in public life, and where necessary should exert their influence to bring changes about.

As a person and an individual, man also has a social and political nature. Personal love thus has an inherent tendency toward its own institutionalization; in this way the freedom of man is organized, infrastructures are created and an appropriate economic and political/administrative system fashioned.

None of this is frowned upon by the ethos of the New Testament, even though the world situation and other contemporary factors that prevailed at the time the Gospels were written understandably gave this ethos at first a community orientation. But even then love for one's neighbor went beyond the community and was manifested in public acts, such as collections to help other churches (2 Cor 8:1–15), the appointment of permanent ministers to distribute alms and practice the works of mercy, and the establishment of diaconates (Rom 12:8; Philemon 1:1). When freedom is constantly threatened, as it is at the present time, and the possibility of living one's life worthily is under constant threat from ideological pressures, the progress of technology, the snares of consumerism, thirst for power at the expense of human dignity and the exploitation of neocolonialism, there is all the more reason and need for social commitment to work for the establishment of structures that are worthy of the human person and of a just social and political order.

Yet this gives our question about the possibility of experiencing faith a quite new dimension: the problem is posed, in other words, whether Christianity's political and social relevance can be revealed to us and convince us, in our quest for faith, and whether social situations or public events are able to assure us of the truth of Revelation in the same way that individual private life can do.

Perhaps the spontaneous assent to the truths of the Faith — "Yes, that's how it is; that's it" — can be found in this sphere too. I am thinking for instance of the many promises of freedom and delivery for the whole People of God in the Old Testament, provided they repented and prayed. In Austria, too, at the end of the last war, there was widespread response to the appeal for such prayer for collective atonement and reparation. An organization pledged to this purpose, with a membership of over two million, still exists today. And Austria, unlike Germany, was spared the threat of a national division and the subjection of a section of the population to Communist neocolonialism. Anyone who looks more closely at the historical situation in question will not be too hasty in claiming that Austria's freedom is due solely to skillful diplomatic negotiation and special strategic circumstances.

One further instance may help throw light on our investigation of whether social and political events are able to lay the foundations for faith in man: I refer to Martin Luther King and his struggle for justice and love using the weapons of non-violence alone.

In January 1956, after surviving an attempt on his life, he managed to calm down an aggressive crowd of black people, but he was full of fear and on the verge of despair. He said to God:

> I am here to fight for a cause that I consider to be just. But I am afraid. The people are urging me to lead them. But if I am weak and fearful, they will also be weak. And I have exhausted my strength. I have reached the point where I can no longer master the situation on my own.[3]

Then he made up his mind: he would not give in. He would go on with this struggle against poverty and the lack of human rights, against the social and political injustice from which the blacks were suffering. He did everything in his power to ensure that they were finally recognized for what they are: people created in the image of God, who wished them to be equal in dignity and before the law to the whites.

On April 4, 1968, the black pastor had to pay the price of his struggle with his own life. He did

[3] From J. P. Delarge, *Prier avec Martin Luther King* (Paris, 1981), 17.

not survive to witness the incontrovertible progress that his movement has achieved in the United States in the fields of law, politics and education, despite all the problems that still remain to be solved. Yet he had clearly been given, like Moses, at least a glimpse of the promised land, and this vision enabled him to overcome his fear and strengthen his faith. On August 28, 1963, addressing a crowd of some 60,000 whites and 200,000 blacks, Martin Luther King declared: "I have a dream that one day my four children may live in a country where they will not be judged by the color of their skin. . . . I have a dream. . . ." His prayers, his struggles, his campaign of nonviolence found a response at least in his dream, and that dream led him to feel, "Yes, that's how it is; that's it."

God's message is also relevant to society and politics. Historical events can often give man the certainty that God is the Lord of history and that his promise is fulfilled in it. Whenever the human person, his dignity and freedom are defended and given the justice due to them at any time in history, then beyond doubt what is at issue here, whatever else one might say on the matter, is the possibility for the people of that time to deepen their faith or find it for the first time.

Yet this possibility is shown, on closer inspection, to be beset by pitfalls: Martin Luther King found it extremely difficult to draw the borderline between his movement and Stokely Carmichael's Black Power movement. Any form of political and social commitment cannot avoid, in other words, taking sides. For those impatient for change, it becomes all too easily enmeshed in the logic of this world, all too easily seduced by the temptation to use every means at their disposal and to rely wholly on force—no matter the cost— to attain their goals.

But should not every possible means be tried if peaceful efforts fail to work? Can the Christian continue to look on passively and see how man is being downtrodden throughout the world? Can he continue to turn a blind eye when the imperialism of the Western economic powers is reducing the poor in the developing countries to ever greater poverty; when black Christians in South Africa are being tortured by racism each day, to the point when they say: "I hate all the whites, and so I hate you, too"; when part of a whole nation is imprisoned behind a wall in Berlin, victim to such oppression that time and again they risk their lives trying to escape, and more than eighty people have already been killed in the attempt; when young practicing Catholics in Northern Ireland, out of political idealism, have opted for suicide through hunger strikes; and when dictatorships in East and West are using systematic torture and compulsory psychiatric treatment to prop up their regimes?

Could anyone animated by the least regard for human dignity possibly keep silent about such crying injustices? And since peaceful methods of removing them have proved ineffective, not a few people feel prompted to resort to violence. They want the gospel of love to become a reality in the world, and yet this same gospel becomes a hindrance: love can come into being for these people only if they break the commandment of love. Justice and peace for one group of people can be achieved, in their judgment, only by the combat and persecution of others.

The effort to achieve faith through experience thus leads to a dilemma, to a cul-de-sac. And the only way out is to ask what Jesus himself did. How did he see himself? What do his life and preaching have to teach us about using violent means to achieve social and political reform? Did he make use of the "power rationale of this world"? A few remarks may at least help toward a possible answer to these questions.

Jesus entered a historical context distinguished, for the Jewish people at large, by grinding oppression, the unspeakable horrors of war and the thwarting of national hopes. Martin Hengel writes:

> No other people of antiquity defended itself so doggedly and relentlessly as did the Jews against the alien influence of hellenistic culture and the oppression to which they were subjected by the Ro-

man domination. As the three abortive revolts of 66–74, 115–117 and 132–135 A.D. show, this resistance almost brought about the destruction of the Jewish people.[4]

Jesus, whose words were often given a political interpretation, could have used his influence over the people to change the established order by force. Just how ripe was the ground for such a violent uprising is shown by the movement of the Zealots.

Jesus, however, did not come to establish a temporal power. He adopted a detached and critical attitude to the political authorities of his time. In the presence of God they were for him stripped of their power. And the individual, no matter his or her state in life, could feel free before them, especially if the mighty were bent on crushing their humanity (see for example Jesus' comments about paying taxes in Mk 12:13ff.). Jesus kept company with the déclassés, with the spurned publicans who exploited the people. He held up the "enemy of the people", the Samaritan, as his model of good conduct, and not the Jewish hereditary nobility, the priests and the Levites. He spoke out harshly against mammon (Lk 16:9ff.) and all feudal structures.

[4] Martin Hengel, *Gewalt und Gewaltlosigkeit* (Stuttgart, 1971), 38ff.

Jesus did not see evil primarily in the transsubjective, in social and political relationships, in the hereditary priesthood, in the powerful landowning class or in the power of Rome itself. He saw it first and foremost in the heart of the individual. His first requirement was therefore a change of heart; he radicalized the Old Testament commandment of love (cf. Lev 19:18) by demanding a boundless willingness to forgive and the repudiation of all forms of hatred.

Jesus was able to demand this boundless love because he knew that man is sustained by the Father's love, which surpasses and overcomes all suffering. This love is shown to be all the stronger if the situation in which man finds himself is unworthy of his dignity and a source of scandal. This trust in the Father absolves the disciple from the need to justify and defend himself, makes him refrain from any aggressive act of vengeance and stops him from glorifying any success he may obtain through unlawful means. Through his trust in the Father, Jesus was free even when confronted by suffering and sacrifice.

Yet this trust can hardly be said to exist if the injustice that reigns in the world leads man to challenge or reject the commandment that he should love *all* his fellowmen because they are his brothers. Any such rejection would mean that, as far as the manifestation of faith through experience is concerned, the actors have secretly changed roles.

Originally, in other words, the gaining of faith through experience was spoken of, because it was *God* who honored his promise and strengthened the faith of the people in this way, i.e., through experience. But such claims overlooked the fact that experience can never provide all that is promised by the Faith for its fulfillment in the hereafter: all that is dismissed, in the terminology of Karl Marx, as "opium". But since man set about his quest to experience all the truths of the Faith (his *Suchprojekt*, to use Schillebeeckx' term), he has come to the conclusion that in some cases he must create for himself the conditions required to enable him to gain such an experience. In his impatience, he is unwilling to wait until redemption be granted; instead, he tries to create it himself. It is hardly surprising if, in this attempt, he should be led to throw in his lot with ideologies of all kinds that promise earthly salvation. For these ideologies too have nothing to look forward to in hope; they only experience the salvation that they themselves bring about on earth.

The thesis of "faith through experience" no doubt has its psychological advantages. For it conforms with the way modern man understands himself. Modern man endeavors to verify assertions, and his own ability to check their truthfulness through his own experience gives him the greatest sense of security. What other people say cannot influence his conviction, for any such "dependence" conflicts with what he sees as his right to self-determination.

As we have seen, however, the thesis that personal experience can provide the basis for faith reveals its limitations when applied to the problem of culture as an aid to faith. Even in the sphere of social commitment, it cannot be given any absolute value.

Let us conclude with a few remarks on its possible role in the sphere of the family.

3. The Family

It is the mother who gives the newborn baby its first experience of love and affection. Through her care and tenderness she calls the child out of its own self-isolation. Her loving smile engenders in the child the knowledge that it is not self-sufficient; that the "I" has to be awakened by the "you"; and that the longings of the human person cannot be satisfied in a condition of stasis or self-satisfaction, as symbolized by the geometrical figure of the circle, but only when the "I" and the "you" "vibrate in the ellipsis of love" (H. U. von Balthasar). It is only when the "I" is accepted by the "you" that the human person becomes aware of himself and able to realize himself: space and the world do not exist thanks to the "I", but solely thanks to the "you". It is the art of the "you", and not the capacity of the "I", that gives the "I" the impetus to set out in its quest for the "you". That is why man is distinguished in his innermost being by the wish to be accepted, recognized and led by affection out of his own self-isolation. And the milieu that fulfills this fundamental need for self-transcendence is the family. Acceptance and affection are the fundamental strengths that sustain the family. They constitute the promise that the family holds out to the individual.

For believers, this gift of love and affection, and the longing to receive it, are quite obvious. For believers can experience and see the way in which transient nature is surrounded by everlasting gifts. They allow themselves to be led on by Jesus Christ, and they recognize the almighty and omnipotent Creator of heaven and earth as their Father, to whom they can say, "Abba, dear Father". For they believe in his boundless love and in the haven that he holds out to them; they have faith in their unconditional acceptance by him. When this God, in his desire to bring them salvation through no merit of their own, reaches out unceasingly toward his Chosen People, he speaks to them not only directly through his Word but through all the experiences of those who give themselves to each other in mutual love; he speaks to them through the experiences of those who taste the ecstasy of falling in love, the experiences of choosing a partner, of becoming engaged and of sharing the life-long bond of marriage in mutual faithfulness.

It is for this very reason that all those forces that build up and sustain the family are better suited to permit the experience of the truths of the Faith than those present in any other sphere of life. It is easier in the family than anywhere else for the believer to reach the conclusion: "Yes, that's how it is; that's it."

Yet it has to be admitted that self-fulfillment and acceptance are not always the responses that the human community holds in store for the longings of the individual. Lovers discover that, in spite of all their goodwill, they are incapable of enduring in their love or fulfilling the hopes they originally inspired in each other. Poets have described their disappointed hopes, their frustrations, their disillusionment and suffering. For example, Paul Claudel, a writer we have already met in these pages, describes, in his *Le Soulier de Satin* (*The Satin Slipper*), how Rodrigue and Prouhèze, after so passionately falling in love, find themselves unable to live up to their hopes or give each other the bliss they had expected. In the whole of Claudel's works, indeed, we find no portrayal of any lasting fulfillment of the relationship between man and woman. In his play *La Ville* he even puts the following words into the mouth of a woman: "I am the promise that cannot be kept."

The costly experience of happiness had proved short-lived and had only fueled desire without quenching it.

Clearly this is due not to any particular misfortune, by accident, so to say. If we listen to another French writer, Léon Bloy, it is precisely this loss of happiness, this painful privation of the hoped-for affection, that provides the very touchstone and proof of genuine love. He writes: "If someone claims to love me but refuses to suffer through me, that person must simply be a usurer of feeling who wants to ply his trade in my heart."

Anyone who agrees with all this—and not only great French writers but our own self-observation confirms it—will find himself placed in a difficult situation when it comes to testing the thesis of whether the truths of the Faith can be revealed through experience: it means that man, as a proof of his love, must be willing to be deprived of affection. If this is so, the believer must start out from the presupposition that God's love will bring him the apparent withdrawal of God's affection, in other words, suffering and spiritual distress. Unfortunately this is an undisputed fact. And yet it has to be recognized that belief in God's goodness and love can hardly ever be founded on the experience of this suffering. For when we experience pain, we can hardly ever be convinced of the redeeming truth of God's love for us. The experience of suffering can hardly ever inspire our spontaneous assent to the Faith or lead us to declare: "Yes, that's how it is; that's it." On the contrary, from Job onward the whole world has rung with the accusations leveled against a God who allows the death of the innocent, who fails to remove dictatorships and torture and looks on with apparent indifference on the spectacle of human misery.

The key word *suffering*, which for the believer means the Cross, shows, in other words, that the thesis that experience forms the basis of faith does not go far enough. It pushes the truth of the Cross into the background, since it is regarded as catechetically difficult, pastorally ineffective and, in any case, no longer suitable for a world in which the teachings of the Gospel are quite happily watered down and reduced to the status of rules for *savoir vivre*. Now as ever, this message of the Cross is "a stumbling block to Jews and folly to Gentiles" (1 Cor 1:23).

Yet this Cross must not be played down by anyone concerned with the question of the foundation or strengthening of the Faith, even though it is not immediately clear to the light of the human intelligence; even though it is beyond the grasp of the feelings and flies in the face of what man is capable of comprehending. The Cross points the way into the abyss of human experience. It epitomizes the experience of darkness and testifies to the power to withstand the remoteness of the "you". It enables us to hear the cry: "My God, my God, why have you forsaken me?'' (Mt 27:46). And yet it is just this cry, the nadir of suffering and the essence of the *nonexperience* of the Faith, which providentially paves the way for man to move forward with God and gives him the grace of faith.

Karl Rahner was one of the first thinkers in our time who has tried to relate the world of human experience to the world of faith. In his article *Erfahrung der Gnade* (1954), Rahner argues that it is not the confirmation given by experience, but the Cross—in other words, our experience of negative phenomena—that provides the basis for the possibility of forging a relationship between man and God. He writes:

> Have we ever kept quiet, even though we wanted to defend ourselves when we had been unfairly treated? Have we ever forgiven someone even though we got no thanks for it and our silent forgiveness was taken for granted? Have we ever obeyed, not because we had to and because otherwise things would have become unpleasant for us, but simply on account of that mysterious, silent, incomprehensible being we call God and his will? Have we ever sacrificed something without receiving any thanks or recognition for it, and even without a feeling of inner satisfaction? Have we ever been absolutely lonely? Have we ever decided on some course of action purely by the innermost judgment of our conscience, deep down where one can no longer tell or explain it to any-

one, where one is quite alone and knows that one is taking a decision which no one else can take in one's place and for which one will have to answer for all eternity? Have we ever tried to love God when we are no longer being borne on the crest of the wave of enthusiastic feeling, when it is no longer possible to mistake our self, and its vital urges, for God? Have we ever tried to love him when we thought we were dying of this love and when it seemed like death and absolute negation? Have we ever tried to love God when we seemed to be calling out into emptiness and our cry seemed to fall on deaf ears, when it looked as if we were taking a terrifying jump into the bottomless abyss, when everything seemed to become incomprehensible and apparently senseless? Have we ever fulfilled a duty when it seemed that it could be done only with a consuming sense of really betraying and obliterating oneself, when it could apparently be done only by doing something terribly stupid for which no one would thank us? Have we ever been good to someone who did not show the slightest sign of gratitude or comprehension and when we also were not rewarded by the feeling of having been "selfless", decent, etc?

Let us search for ourselves in such experiences in our life; let us look for our own experiences in which things like this have happened to us individually. If we find such experiences, then we have experienced the Spirit in the way meant here. For the experience meant here is the experience of eternity; it is the experience that the Spirit is more than merely a part of this temporal world; the experience that man's meaning is not exhausted by the meaning and fortune of this world; the experience of the adventure and confidence of taking the plunge, an experience which no longer has any reason which can be demonstrated or which is taken from the success of this world.[5]

In conclusion, our thinking today, as influenced by contemporary trends, is, as I have already said, very much in line with the proposition that faith can be grounded through experience. In presenting the argument put forward by Edward Schillebeeckx, we thus examined our own modern mentality. And in the course of this examination, a certain amount of scepticism emerged about the reliability and soundness of Christian experience. What modern Christians hold to be true from their own experience can often not be unreservedly confirmed by a deeper analysis of the Faith. Indeed, a dialectic emerged on at least three points in the course of our examination, and this dialectic means that we have to answer both "yes" and "no" to the dictates of experience: to the spontaneous judgment of human reason, no matter how firmly based on an informed Christian conscience.

1. The task of working jointly for the construction of society and the well-being of daily life by

[5] Karl Rahner, *Schriften zur Theologie*, vol. 33, 2d ed. (Einsiedeln, 1957), 105–9, here 106.

fostering the dignity of the human person and the value of culture is essentially the duty of the laity. Forms of life and signs of the Faith need to be promoted to prevent the Christian's conviction from wavering. We need to preserve or strive toward spheres of freedom in which Christian life can be lived. Yet it is only to be expected that many attempts by individuals or by groups to do so will end in failure, because the secularized environment in which they necessarily operate will crush them. When this happens, Christians must not lose hope; they must be patient and long-suffering; they must not be discouraged in their commitment. Failure is not a catastrophe. The action of God's Spirit is not bound to external signs or particular places. Indeed, sometimes these signs and places may even be a stumbling block themselves: "The wind blows where it wills," says Christ in Saint John's Gospel, "and you hear the sound of it, but you do not know whence it comes or whither it goes" (Jn 3:8).

2. Many things that appear to people as crosses are, in fact, abuses, against which our reaction is necessary. We must strive, by protest and resistance, to change them. Yet, in the last analysis, the Cross cannot be removed or eradicated from human life. Any system of coordinates in which no room is left for the Cross as a basis for our judgment and action must be rejected. When difficulties or disasters strike at us or at others, we must at

least try to give them some meaning; they are the means of bringing redemption, and even though beyond our grasp or inaccessible to our experience, they bring grace and salvation. Nevertheless, most of us will always find it difficult to say with Saint Paul: "I rejoice in my sufferings for your sake" (Col 1:24).

3. It is the duty of Christians too to create righteousness and justice in the world. How this can be achieved, and how we can play a part in it, often, however, remain beyond our insight. Faith alone can sustain our hope in an eternal reward. Yet this element of "opium" in our Christian faith is not to be frowned on. The apostle Paul tells us: "Eye has not seen, ear has not heard, nor has it so much as dawned on man what God has prepared for those who love him" (1 Cor 2:9).

IV

MODERN DEMOCRACY AND THE COMMON PRIESTHOOD OF ALL THE FAITHFUL

Currents of ideas undoubtedly exist in history that transcend the frontiers of countries and continents. They are transmitted from one group of people to another and exert a more or less strong influence, whether temporary or long-lasting. These currents of ideas have a significant influence on our decisions and conduct.

If problems like the spirituality and sociopolitical commitment of the lay associations and movements are considered today, then due attention must be paid to a perceptible spiritual movement that influences man's thinking on a worldwide scale: namely, the ideal of democracy as a model of human society and community. This ideal enduringly characterizes both the spiritual orientation and sociopolitical commitment of the lay communities in the Church today.

1. The Influence of Movements of Ideas on the Faith

The Word of God is given to man once and for all. It is not exchangeable, nor does it admit amendment or supplementation. Even though it was determined by a clearly defined geographical area and had its origin in a quite specific historical epoch, it nonetheless retains its universal validity for all men and for all time. The Word of God thus has absolute qualities; it became flesh and dwelt among us. It was incarnated once and for all in the person of the Eternal Word (cf. Jn 1).

Yet if we were to conclude from the uniqueness and unrepeatability of the Word of God that it should be allowed quietly to atrophy, to become fossilized through the process of history, we would be ignoring its true character. We would be turning tradition into conservatism; the Word of God would become mummified by an alleged fidelity to the transmission of a deformed version of it. God addressed himself to his creation in human speech in order to win us to himself. But the patina of age and the monotony of habit are obstacles, and not aids, to this end. Both impede man's readiness to accept the Gospel and its power to convince, even though it remains true that every new form of expressing the Good News must not tamper with the truth of God's Word.

The "translation" of the biblical tradition into a particular historical situation is in the first place a linguistic question, a matter of terminology and syntax: the Hebrew text was first translated into Greek, this in turn into Latin and so on. Yet the transmission of the Revelation requires more than new linguistic formulations. Only superficially is a language determined by vocabulary and style alone. We find, on closer inspection, that it is elucidated by comparisons and illusions; that it uses images and experiences; that it assimilates new ways of thinking, new ways of life. In this way it takes cognizance of what is new and coins terms to express them. It constantly opens up new possibilities so as to penetrate ever more deeply into what it has to express. Language can thus contribute to formulating eternal truths in ways appropriate to the time, and so make them more "current".

The truth of the Revelation and of the progagation of the Word of God are also deepened by the forms of Church life that animate the Faith. These forms are continuously influenced by the stimuli given by the particular society in which they operate. The Church has never categorically rejected the models of life of the world by which she is surrounded: on the contrary, she verifies and holds onto "what is good" (1 Th 5:21). This attitude to the surrounding world is a consequence of the vocation of the Church herself and her wish to be incarnated in the society in which she operates. The fact that the Church has been willing to be stimulated in this way has been of great help to the faithful by shaping an ecclesial order consonant with their times; for the social structures of a particular historical period generally have greater relevance and appeal for the people living in it. It can therefore be only to the advantage of the Church's pastoral ministry if the preachers and interpreters of the Gospel are familiar with, and pay heed to, the mentality of their time. The less the "language" of the Faith is redolent of the atmosphere of the ghetto, the more likely it will be to be understood and accepted by contemporaries. Hence, the attempt to explain the truths of the Faith in the light of modern attitudes and conduct is worth the trouble. Otherwise the very content of the Faith would risk being rendered obsolescent by an alien language and outmoded models.

The fact that the Church sees herself confronted by the idea of democracy today provides a concrete example of what is at issue in the above reflections. Democratic principles are accorded a high value today and visibly mark our mentality. As a consequence, efforts have not been lacking, especially since the Second Vatican Council, to bring the postive contents of this political order to bear also on the life of the Church herself.

Theological reflection on this influence, which is making itself felt in many places, has been able to identify a surprising degree of affinity between fundamental biblical concepts and democratic ideas. In what follows, these similarities will be examined in more detail. The purpose of this examination will be to see whether the essential elements of the Church's structure, as predetermined by the Revelation itself, are capable of being harmed by the adoption of democratic thinking.

2. "Liberty, Equality and Fraternity" as the Fundaments of the Democratic Way of Life

The affinity of biblical thought with the idea of democracy can first be shown by their respective evaluations of *liberty*. There is no doubt that we all approve of the independence and freedom of citizens from forcibly imposed foreign power. The best of all possible situations in life is self-determination: man's freedom to determine his own destiny. Amnesty International is at most criticized for partisanship, but never for its basic purpose.

Such fundamental ideas, however, directly impinge on the Christian view of the freedom of the children of God. Far from wanting to curtail, still less repress, freedom, the Gospel and the Church want to bring it about; they want to foster and strengthen it. The New Testament references to the liberating impulse of the gift of salvation are many (cf. Gal 2:4: "our freedom which we have in Christ Jesus", and elsewhere). Whoever hands himself over and lets himself succumb to the bondage of any kind of enslaving power loses not only his independence, but also the Gospel and his human dignity.

Second, the *equality* of human beings, the removal of gross disparities among them, seems to us a laudable goal today. It remains incomprehensible to us that inherited privileges should continue to bolster classes and castes or that women should be paid less for their work for no other reason than they are not men. Already in the democracy of the Greek *polis*, the commonwealth was regarded as supported by a community of equals. Both privileged and subservient orders were regarded as abolished. The democratic system was so devised to ensure that no particular persons and groups could monopolize the decision-making process; indeed, it was aimed at giving civil rights and equal opportunities precisely to the weaker members of society.

The New Testament also speaks of equality: the equality of all men and women in Christ. Thus, Paul writes in his Letter to the Galatians:

> In Christ Jesus you are all sons of God through faith. For as many of you were baptized into Christ have put on Christ. There is neither Jew nor Greek, there is neither slave nor free, there is neither male nor female; for you are all one in Christ Jesus.
>
> — Gal 3:26–28

By sonship in Jesus Christ, therefore, the differences between peoples and confessions, between civil rank and gender, have been abolished (cf. also

James 2:2–4). The preaching of Jesus himself also emphasized this concept of equality, as when he forbade his disciples and the whole people from calling someone rabbi because they had only *one* teacher, or from calling someone father, "for you have one Father who is in heaven" (Mt 23:8–9).

Thirdly, *fraternity*: men are bound together into a brotherhood by equality with their fellowmen. It was not just during the French Revolution that this consequence of equality was discovered. For already the Athenian democracy had promised, at least as far as its own *polis* was concerned, that the members of the commonwealth should be able to realize their common humanity in brotherhood and cooperate together in benevolence, mutual care and solicitude. Plato calls fellow-citizens of the *polis* "brother", and Xenophon calls them "friend". Kinship was thus extended to the people as a whole. On the other hand, personal bonds were forged through affection according to the principle of "elective affinties".[1] Admittedly, our own age no longer sings along with Friedrich Schiller: "*Seid umschlungen, Millionen . . .*" (his rousing paean to universal brotherhood), but man today is no less receptive if the right signals of trust and acceptance are made to him. Many people

[1] Cf. J. Ratzinger, *Christliche Brüderlichkeit* (Munich, 1960), 12.

seek the experience of brotherhood in our time, and have found it in novel social associations and in groups of the most varied type. That this aspiration corresponds with Christian teaching can be shown by numerous New Testament quotations. Here I will only point out the consequence drawn by the Lord from the fact that we all have a common Father in heaven: "you are all brothers" (Mt 23:8).

Similar is that other saying of Jesus, in his reaction to the announcement of the visit of his mother and brothers:

> "Who are my mother and my brothers?" And looking around on those who sat about him, he said, "here are my mother and my brothers! Whoever does the will of God is my brother, and sister, and mother."
>
> — Mk 3:34–35

Jesus himself saw kinship no longer in terms of a relationship of blood, but of spirit.

These biblical verses show that the fundamental elements of democracy do have their correspondence in the Revelation. And yet they do not simply coincide with the gifts given to Christians through Christ. Jesus, on the contrary, went beyond the natural law. He chose a better standpoint, for he had a new point of reference: the Father and his will. This fact should simply be noted here.

3. The Common Priesthood of All the Faithful and the New Testament Definition of Priesthood

The distinguishing features of democracy — liberty, equality and fraternity — reflect in some way what it is that determines the rank of Christians and what it is that distinguishes Christian life. Less differentiated than in the secular world, bundled together as it were, these criteria recur in both the Old and New Testament under the guise of the concept of the "common priesthood". This concept became a kind of key word at the Second Vatican Council, and one that was used to propagate the democratic principles of liberty, equality and fraternity in the Church. Yet a more exhaustive investigation of the concept of the "common priesthood" shows that this biblical teaching contains a good deal more than a mere confirmation of democratic principles through Revelation.

In the First Letter of Peter, the faithful are exhorted "to be a holy priesthood to offer spiritual sacrifices acceptable to God through Jesus Christ". They are declared to be "a chosen race, a royal priesthood, a holy nation that they might declare the wonderful deeds of him who called them out of darkness into his wonderful light" (1 Pet 2:5, 9).

These declarations form the culmination and conclusion of the exhortation in the initial part of the First Letter of Peter. They are indicative of the promise of salvation, which receives its justification only in the imperative of carrying out the work of salvation. Both verses stand parallel to each other and serve a single purpose. Both derive their foundation from a passage in the Old Testament (Ex 19:4ff.). The sense of the New Testament statement is revealed all the more clearly if that of the Old Testament passage on which it is based is considered. The passage in question reads:

> You have seen what I did to the Egyptians, and how I bore you on eagles' wings and brought you to myself. Now therefore, if you will obey my voice and keep my covenant, you shall be my own possession among all peoples; for all the earth is mine, and you shall be to me a kingdom of priests and a holy nation.
>
> — Ex 19:4–6

In this key passage, God promised the children of Israel, at the beginning of their sojourn in the wilderness of Sinai, that they were the Chosen People. The bitter experience of Israel in the bondage of Egypt formed the background to this choice. Yahweh reversed this experience, and led Israel out of Egypt. On condition that this once-subjugated people remain true to Yahweh, the Lord offered it a covenant. Israel thus became God's "own possession among all peoples", not the possession of the mundane world; for the whole of the creation belonged to the Lord in any case. Rather, Israel was to be for Yahweh something unique and precious: something that a king could call his own. God's promise of a covenant to Moses in Sinai enables us to gain a first idea of what is meant by the "common priesthood": it is the fruit of Yahweh's initiative of salvation. Yahweh offered a covenant and created it, even before Israel herself could begin to fulfill her part of the bargain. He gathered together his people from its almost annihilated remnant in Egypt. The Lord then led this people out of bondage into the promised land, and at the same time separated it from other peoples, so that it might be a sign of salvation. The holiness of the people is thus inseparably bound up with its choice by Yahweh to be his "own possession among all peoples".

The same premise is implicit in the New Testament designation of the "royalty" of the priesthood (cf. 1 Pet 2:9). This people was pledged to the King of Kings; and because of this pledge to God the King, it achieved royal status.

Yet indisputably the main significance of the New Testament text is that God's initiative of salvation should be *praised*. The passage from the First Letter of Peter in question is especially to be interpreted as an exhortation to the worship and praise of God's action by which the Chosen People had been called "out of darkness into his wonderful light". The repercussions of this initiative naturally had an effect on the people as such, but these consequences are only touched on. For the authors of the Bible are still immune from modern egocentrism and anthropocentrism, which narcissistically portray everything in terms purely of its reaction on the self and on people in general and push God into the background as the source and origin of all human dignity and enhancement.

In the biblical text, the theocentrism of the statement can be grasped from the way it spells out the consequences of being the Chosen People: the offering of spiritual sacrifices (1 Pet 2:5) and the proclamation of the wonderful deeds of God (1 Pet 2:9) are declared to be the duties of the people of God.

Spiritual sacrifice, *thysia*, is in the New Testament too, the offering of gifts. But it is through the acceptance of God's will, and not (as in the Old Testament) through the *representative* or vicarious gift, that God is worshipped or reconciled in the New Covenant. The individual is himself called on to accept God's will. *Thysia* is thus an act of obedience signifying self-dedication to God and submission to his will. It is characterized in the First Letter of Peter as "spiritual", since an offering, if it is to be acceptable to God and his Spirit, demands a force that transcends all human measure.

This real dedication to God and our fellowmen takes the form of the proclamation of the wonderful deeds of God to the surrounding world. The believer does not seek his own self-interest or his own honor in making this spiritual sacrifice: it is by praising God's gift of salvation, and not by serving his own self, that he fulfills his God-given duty. The process of salvation can thus be summarized as follows: God chooses his people, who dedicate themselves to the praise of the greatness of God through a life lived in accordance with their covenant with him. The priesthood of the faithful bear witness, by their transformation in Christ, to him who called them out of darkness into his wonderful light.

What is meant by the Christian understanding of brotherhood is shown even more clearly by the biblical definition of priesthood. The Revelation is conceived and formulated in a decidedly theocentric way; the priesthood too is therefore to be construed in a theocentric light, i.e., one that is constantly related to and derived from God. Priesthood is not something that belongs to the community of the faithful or something that has, through their action, become their possession. Our current conception of the role of the priest thus needs at least to be amplified if we are to take the biblical interpretation as its basis. For a priest is generally conceived by us today as someone who offers sacrifice, even if this naturally has its presuppositions. The quality of being a priest is thus understood by us primarily as an aptitude for a certain kind of activity, not as something that is, in origin, passively received. As defined in this sense—a special aptitude or ability to offer sacrifice distinguishing one person from another—the role of the priest was even enshrined in the resolutions of the Council of Trent (DS 1764).

An examination of another New Testament text, the Letter to the Hebrews, makes it clear, however, that priesthood is not in fact identical with the role or qualification of being able to offer sacrifice. For this letter explicitly confirms the feature we have already emphasized: that priesthood means in the first place being chosen by God.

According to the Letter to the Hebrews, there is only one person who deserves the name of priest in the full sense: Jesus Christ himself. This Jesus Christ fulfilled his priesthood by dedicating himself wholly to the will of God to the point of offering his own blood in sacrifice (Heb 9:11f.; 10:7). But not even the Lord derived his priesthood in the first place from his own action: he was given it by the initiative of God, by having been chosen by God. Christ, says the Letter to the Hebrews, "did not exalt himself to be made a high priest, but was appointed by him who said to him, 'Thou art my Son, today I have begotten thee.' " And it was by this appointment, by this choice, that Christ became "a priest for ever, after the order of Melchizedek" (Heb 5:5). Christ's priesthood thus derives its foundation from God's action, from his having been appointed through God's Word.

The reference to King Melchizedek in the passage we have just quoted reinforces the notion that Christ's priesthood, and indeed every priesthood, derives its origin from the salvific initiative of God. This flows from the following considerations: communities in the Jewish tradition naturally started out (also in the first century A.D.) from the assumption that their ability for cult service was derived by priestly descent. The author of the Letter to the Hebrews was now faced with the task of convincing these communities that Christ was a priest, although he could point to no such lineage in support of it. He thus enlisted the aid of Melchizedek. Melchizedek, king of Salem, is described in the Old Covenant as priest of the Most High God, even though his ancestry could provide no foundation for any such priesthood. He was "without father or mother or genealogy" (Heb 7:3). The king of Salem thus became the type of priest whose priesthood was not derived from man. The author of the Letter to the Hebrews completes his comparison through an interpolation of a verse from Psalm 110 ("The Lord has sworn and will not change his mind, 'You are a priest for ever after the order of Melchizedek' ") and so ensures that the similarity of the two priests will redound to the invincible superiority of

Christ; God himself founded the priesthood of Christ by his own Word. When the writer of the letter calls Christ "priest after the order of Melchizedek", he thus means to say: neither the place in a genealogical tree nor appointment by man provides the foundation of the priesthood of Christ. His priesthood is without blemish, for Christ is a priest forever after the order of Melchizedek; in other words, he was begotten by God and designated a priest by God.

If we want to interpret the basic principles of democracy in biblical terms, the biblical teaching on the "common priesthood" takes us a long way. Liberty, equality and fraternity are all implicit in it. First, the freedom of the Christian is accurately conveyed by the liberation from the bondage of Egypt and of sin that is expressed by the biblical teaching on the common priesthood. Second, equality, understood in the Christian way, derives from the equal portion of the royalty of God that God grants to all his people. And third, brotherhood in Christ is realized in the Church and the community by the selfless commitment of the children of God, which, according to the First Letter of Peter, consists in proclaiming God's salvation and declaring to the world the wonderful deeds of him who called them out of darkness.

To sum up, an examination of the First Letter of Peter shows that the reality of the common priesthood is in the first place derived from its expressly theocentric nature. This derivation from God is the decisive factor of all priesthood, as is explicitly confirmed by the Letter to the Hebrews.

Yet in spite of the approximation between political and theological ideas, the question as to the new interpretation of the concept of "democracy" still awaits a satisfactory answer. On closer inspection, this question reveals a further problem. In attempting to elucidate it we must tackle the intellectual foundations of modern democracy.

4. Modern Democracy:
A Secular Derivation from the
Biblical Message of the Common Priesthood

According to the constitutionalist (and later federal constitutional judge in the Federal Republic of Germany) Gerhard Leibholz, the tradition of Western democratic thought was substantially determined by Christianity and humanism.[2] In origin, therefore, modern democracy shares common ground with Christianity; indeed, it is Leibholz's conviction that modern democracy is inconceivable without Christianity.

If we look into the question more closely, we find that the roots of modern democracy can be

[2] Gerhard Leibholz, *Das Wesen der Repräsentation und der Gestaltwandel der Demokratie im 20 Jahrhundert* (Berlin, 1966), 211.

traced back to England. In the time of Cromwell
(d. 1658) the Puritans abandoned England and
sailed to a new home in North America; they took
with them the beginnings of democratic thought
and adapted them to their form of social life. Initially, they placed their "covenants"—their gov-
erning bodies, which also played a political role—
under the sovereignty of God. Similarly, a process
of the conversion of the truths of the Revelation
into political and social forms simultaneously began in England, and it was specifically the idea of
"common priesthood" that lay at the basis of this
conversion. Thus, the form of democracy conceived according to this model was initially conceived as embodying "a religious and moral
principle". First applied to the covenants, this
principle was later extended to the government of
the state as the people became progressively in-
volved in the holding of power. The new form of
government still had its point of reference in religion. Yet an important step in its development
needs to be pointed out: if the new concept of state
government was borrowed in substance from the
Revelation, it became independent in application
and gradually became removed from its original
religious context. This significant transformation
can especially be gauged in the use of a new language. The first creation of modern democracy in
the Anglo-American area has thus been defined
precisely as the "transposition of the spiritual

priesthood of all the faithful into a nontheological language".[3]

As far as England is concerned, the Anglican church has maintained to this day a religious system as a state institution; the English crown has likewise preserved its form as a monarchy whose legitimacy stems from the church. Yet outside England, the Revelation as the context and seedbed of democratic thought was totally eclipsed. It did not survive the conversion of the common priesthood into "nontheological language". God as a point of reference was progressively weakened and abandoned. Since the French Revolution, written constitutions in Europe (if one leaves out of consideration the Bonn Constitution) have deliberately eschewed any invocation of God. The people and humanity have been invoked as points of reference in his stead. The sovereignty of God was replaced by the sovereignty of the people. The declaration of the equality of all men before God was turned into that of the equality of all men before a humanly determined act of will, namely, the law.

This development was a gradual one, spread over several centuries. It did not come with an earth-shattering detonation, but almost without noise. Yet the fundamental change it brought about must not be overlooked. The biblical find-

[3] Ibid.

ings clearly show that the understanding and content of the common priesthood stand and fall with God as the basic axiom. In the democratic thought of the modern period, which is no other than the common priesthood formulated in non-theological language, God, on the contrary, has first been suppressed and then forgotten. Secularization has taken place: from a late Gothic vault, the heavy and elaborately carved keystone has been wrenched out. It is not only the esthetic appeal of the architecture that suffers from this: its very stability has been destroyed. If the keystone held together by its weight all the other structural elements—flying buttresses, ribs, walls—its removal must necessarily involve the whole building in collapse.

These interrelations between the secular and religious worlds caution us with particular clarity against unreflectively applying the basic democratic structure to forms and institutions inside the Church. For it would be presumable that efforts aimed at democratization would lead to the Church adopting a mode of thought exclusively molded by state practices and social customs.

Nor can the undeniable fact be gainsaid that democratic ballots and popular referenda do not necessarily lead to ethically right or even ethically good decisions. Often, indeed, what contributes to the well-being of life is no longer capable of winning a majority in democratic systems. This fundamental proviso, however, should not detract from the fact that joint responsibility for the witness and building up of the Church does require the broad participation of all those baptized and confirmed, and that a meaningful evaluation of this participation for the well-being and growth of the community must be sought.

Moreover, the fact that an atheistic, godless heritage has been concealed in modern democracy since its origin may also have made itself felt, not only in political life but in our faith. For a democratizing trend would then be a contributing factor in our inability to realize God, an inability from which we suffer not only as citizens but also as members of the Church. Anyone who examines the state of theological studies is bound to concede that this inability has substantially increased in the recent past.

As long ago as 1920, the Protestant theologian Friedrich Gogarten published an essay called *Zwischen den Zeiten*, in which he posed the question:

> Do people even exist today who are capable of really conceiving of God? We are all so deeply immersed in our human being that we have lost all trace of God. Yes, really lost; there is no further thought in us that reaches up to him. None of our thoughts reaches beyond our human ken. No, not one.

Yet from this analysis of the secularization of man Gogarten does not draw the conclusion that

God must be proclaimed all the more resolutely and decisively. On the contrary, he responds to man's godlessness by attempting to develop a wholly secularized "theology". It starts out from the assumption that man received the sonship of God in Jesus Christ and that this sonship is the only relationship and the only justification that binds man to God. The creation, seen in this light, has no transcendental nature. The world is mundane, and man is appointed to have autonomous dominion over it, with no need for God. For the world, Gogarten argues, is independent of any religious forces; consequently every sacred interpretation of the world must be rejected—holy places, holy times, holy persons do not exist in the world. The son, whom God made responsible and hence his own master, shaped the world in a worldly way, in absolute profanity. Profane action as a whole has nothing to do with salvation or justification. It takes place in utter isolation from God, in a context of complete secularism. Faith and Revelation are hence without any relevance for coping with life.

Such, in brief, is the theology of Friedrich Gogarten, and in it we can study the logical consequence of a secularized Christianity, a community order abstracted from God. Nor is Gogarten alone in this field: he has a crowd of comrades-in-arms. Here it will suffice to mention them only by a few titles of their books: *End of Religion, Death of God Theology, Absence of God, Atheist Belief in God.* According to these and similar publications and the ideas propagated in them, atheism can also become the natural horizon of a so-called theological system. It should be no cause for surprise, therefore, if individual fields of the Church's pastoral ministry or Church life should be imbued with secularistic ideas and more or less clearly divested of any reference to God.

It is only with the greatest caution, therefore, that secularized interpretations of reality, interpretations stripped of any reference to God, be they philosophical or political, psychological or sociological, should be adopted for theological thought and ecclesial structures. With their religious neutrality, such interpretations are not the useful aids that theology should make grateful use of. They are more likely to lead to a deformation of the Christian interpretation of the origin of the world and of the primacy of God over man, a deformation caused by a system of thought in which the renunciation of any reference to God forms an essential part of its method.

This does not mean that Christians should renounce all aids that propose secular experiences and the findings of modern science for the ordering of everyday life; that would be stupid and would also involve the need to isolate Christians from modern thought and knowledge.

What we should hold onto is the fact that anthropological approaches always contain scales of values, which must be laid open, and if necessary criticized, in the light of the Faith. If we take the Gospel of Jesus Christ as our criterion, then humanistic or scientific models of interpretation must all be exposed to the criticizing, stimulating and integrating potential of Christ's life, death and Resurrection. This does not imply the omnipotence of theology; rather, it means an attentive and serious dialogue on what the individual sciences are able to contribute to the well-being of human life in the light of the Revelation of God in Jesus Christ. Yet in itself the comparison I have offered between democratic thought and analogous biblical teaching has shown that due caution is necessary.

V

COMMUNIO IN THE CHURCH: TOWARD A THEOCENTRIC UNDERSTANDING OF UNITY

People indelibly marked like us by the individualistic thought of the modern period have difficulty identifying or empathizing with the community consciousness of Revelation and the early Church. Yet it is worth investigating the biblical and patristic texts on the Church as community, not only because of the recognized hunger for community felt by people in our time, but also because an investigation of this kind enables us to discover fundamental statements about the nature of Christian life and hence about our own understanding of ourselves as believers.

Community in the Church has roots in the Old Testament, and the Old Testament heritage in the early Church demanded that consideration be given to the Chosen People's consciousness of belonging together: a cohesion represented by the metaphor of the cooperation of the various members of the human body. Exegetes have defined this consciousness in terms of the concept of "corporative personality",[1] and tell us that it is only against this background that the biblical teaching of the common priesthood of the faithful (1 Pet 2:5) can properly be understood.

1. The Threatened Unity of the Early Church

Yet it is not our purpose here to develop the significant *Theoloumenon* of the corporate personality for the treatment of our theme. Rather, we want to let ourselves be guided by the Acts of the Apostles. This account of the initial period of the Church emphasizes, from its very beginning, the unity and unanimity of the newborn community. Thus, it says of their meeting together in the upper room in Jerusalem, after the ascension of the Lord: "All these with one accord devoted themselves to prayer, together with the women and Mary the mother of Jesus" (Acts 1:14). And the introduction to the account of Pentecost reads: "When the day of Pentecost had come, they were all together in one place" (Acts 2:1). What was given its foundation in this way contains an important criterion in unanimity; again and again Luke emphasizes this unanimity: in the prayer of the original community for fearlessness in preaching the Gospel

[1] J. de Fraine, *Adam und seine Nachkommen* (Cologne, 1962).

(Acts 4:24); in the reference to their possessing everything in common (Acts 4:32); in the account of their worship together in Solomon's portico (Acts 5:12); in the prayer of the Church that brought about the liberation of Peter from prison (Acts 12:5–12) and so on.

In itself, the enumeration of the situations that describe the bonds that held the first Christians together enables us to perceive that their inner unity is not to be understood as a reaction to external pressure. The unity of the early Church was ensured neither by the solidarity of mutual assistance at the time of the persecution of the Christians, nor by group interest aimed at guaranteeing the continued existence and growth of the Church. Unity was achieved, rather, by turning toward God and, in the course of the events described in the Acts of the Apostles, was ever more clearly expressed in the opening to the Holy Spirit. It is only at the conclusion to the account of Pentecost that the cooperation of this Spirit is given clear contours. The Acts of the Apostles summarizes the consequences of the pentecostal event as follows:

> They devoted themselves to the Apostles' teaching and fellowship, to the breaking of bread and the prayers . . . and all who believed were together, and had all things in common. . . . And the Lord added to their number day by day those who were being saved.
>
> — Acts 2:42, 44, 47

Community thus reigned among the first Christians by virtue of the strength of the Spirit by which they were filled at Pentecost. And this Spirit, by its very nature, created a unity not self-satisfied and static, but dynamic and missionary.

Yet this gradual growth of the community makes it clear that unity was no secure or unthreatened possession. Indeed, the account of the early Church in the Acts of the Apostles is full of references to the threats and dangers by which unanimity was beset. Members betrayed the truth of the Gospel in their lives and so endangered the life of the community.

Two aspects of this threat to the community particularly stand out. First, there was the problem of splits or schisms. Paul encountered this problem *inter alia* in the community of Corinth. He refers to it in the introductory chapter of his First Letter to the Corinthians. Evidently, dissension among the Christians of Corinth had led to the formation of different groups, divided between each other, and each group claimed to serve different leaders: Paul, Apollos and Cephas are all named. Quarrels and divisions, which even affected the celebration of the Eucharist (1 Cor 11:18), were the result. Paul sharply attacks these schismatic groups. He exerted his authority and expected total submission. As he had done in other communities founded by him, he exhorted the Corinthians to be obedient.

He tried to convince them by examining the mentality and outlook of the sectarians. They identified the Gospel with a personally experienced charismatic word. They thus succumbed to the seduction and self-satisfaction of the wisdom of man (cf. 1 Cor 1:18–19). They were blinded by the worldly logic of empiricism and reason. The Gospel had been transformed for them into a transparent system in which there was no longer any mystery or darkness left. It was comprehensible and could be demonstrated even to outsiders.

These enthusiasts did not want to acknowledge the "folly" of the Gospel: for "God chose what is foolish in the world to shame the wise" (1 Cor 1:27). They did not want to accept the "secret and hidden wisdom" of God which "is not the wisdom of this age or of the rulers of this age" (1 Cor 2:6ff.). It was not the crucified Lord who determined their way of thinking. They were therefore, at bottom, without expectations, without any openness toward God. Or as Paul puts it: "Already you are filled! Already you have become rich! Without us you have become kings!" (1 Cor 4:8). The meeting with the crucified Lord would warn them against wishing to make the Gospel self-serving; it would teach them to let themselves be guided ever anew by God. And they would then be ready to wait, and to accept the whole provisional nature of Christianity:

To receive concretely and not be annoyed with the scantiness of the concrete gift, to thank God really in the way he chose, and to regard God in every respect and in earnest as the source of their life (1 Cor 1:30): that was something that the Corinthian enthusiasts found difficult.[2]

The other danger that threatened unity in the early Church is already implicit in this. But this time the threat was not posed by a group that closed its eyes to the proclamation of the death of Christ on the Cross, to the preaching of the sovereignty of God from the Cross. In this case, men closed their eyes instead to the Good News proclaimed by the risen Christ in history. Chapter 15 of the Acts of the Apostles, for instance, explains the problem. And once again it was Paul who combatted the threat to unity. He accused the community of Jerusalem of trying to put a yoke on the spreading of the Gospel among the Gentiles. The controversy gave rise to the first Council. In the forefront of the debate was the question whether the disciples of Christ had to undergo circumcision and submit to the law of Moses. Yet with this question the world significance of the Christian faith was at stake. For the Jerusalem Council gave the impetus to ensure that the group around Paul did not wither away into a Gentile

[2] H. Schlier, "Die Einheit der Kirche im Denken des Apostels Paulus", in *Die Zeit der Kirche* (Freiburg, 1966), 287–99, here 297.

sect. The union between Jews and Gentiles was forged, and even the Gentiles recognized the Old Testament as their Bible. Thus, the Gentiles were not just entrusted with the pneumatic image of Christ disseminated by Paul: the Palestinian tradition of the earthly life of Jesus was also transmitted to the Gentile Church.

In Jerusalem the decision against provincialism and fossilization, against the timid clinging to outmoded forms, was made. The Apostles recognized from the reaction of the Gentiles to Paul's preaching that God did not want to make the practice of the Jewish law a condition for acceptance of his salvation. His ways are indeed various and not to be encompassed by human plans. Decisive responsibility remained of course with the Twelve; the authority of personal leadership could not be relinquished in the Church. But this had to submit itself to the new and make room for unexpected variety.

> The true Church exists only where both are to be found: legitimacy in the rightful succession to "the Twelve", who directly derived their authority from the Lord; and a faith which, as was also necessary for "the Twelve Apostles", is based on the free decisions of the Holy Spirit. Neither of these characteristics must be lacking: neither the rightful legitimacy nor the peneumatic freedom.[3]

[3] E. Peterson, "Die Kirche", in *Theologische Traktate* (Munich, 1951), 409–24, here 420f.

The evangelist Luke does not fail to ascribe the victory over the danger of ossification to the Holy Spirit. This Spirit had testified that the Gentiles had been won to the Faith. And it was he too who provided the solution to the problem of dissension: "It has seemed good to the Holy Spirit and to us" (Acts 15:28) is the expression used in the letter sent to the community in Antioch. Unity was thus ensured once again; and it was preserved because those holding authority based themselves not on their own prejudices and prepossessions, not on established habits and convictions, but on the impetus that comes from God.

2. *Communio* as God's Sharing of Himself

The concept of God as the guarantor of unity, as the force that heals division, can be developed further and made more precise. This brings us in turn to a concept that has already been implicit in what we have been saying, if not explicitly named: *communio*, or in Greek *koinonia*.

That this concept is of the greatest actuality in our time is testified by many statements of theologians and bishops. It also constituted one of the key ecclesiological concepts of the Extraordinary Synod of Bishops in 1985. The final report reads:

The ecclesiology of communion is a central and fundamental idea of the documents of the Council. *Koinonia*/communion, based on sacred Scripture, was held in great honor in the ancient Church and is so held in the Eastern Churches right up to our time. (C 1)

It is just at this point in our discussion that the concept of *communio* needs to be referred to. For it marks the point at which we need to rethink our ideas about how to preserve the unity of the Church. Hitherto we have mainly been concerned with human efforts aimed at the elimination of division and discord—a mode of thought that seems current, indeed the only one that seems valid, in our time. Yet the concept of *communio*, by contrast, expresses the fundamental truth that unity is not something produced by or derived from man. Unity can arise in the Church, but only as something that the Church cannot create from her own structure. It stems from God: it is not the result of the Church's own efforts.

In its original sense *communio* means "sharing, or participation, in the same means of salvation: in the one Spirit, the one Gospel, the one baptism and the one Eucharist". The foundation for the unity of the faithful lies in the Trinity: our communion with God through Jesus Christ in the Holy Spirit. As the final report of the Extraordinary Synod puts it:

This communion exists through the Word of God and the sacraments. Baptism is the door and foundation of the Church's communion; the Eucharist is the source of the whole of Christian life and its summit. Communion with the Body of Christ in the Eucharist signifies and brings about, or builds up, the intimate union of all the faithful in the Body of Christ, which is the Church. (C 1)

Communio sanctorum is first the sharing in God's gifts of grace (*sancta*) and then the communion with those sanctified in God (*sancti*). In all this, *communio* is participation in divine life.[4] Origen says the following about *communio*:

> If we are given communion with Father and Son and with the Holy Spirit, we must take care not to place ourselves in opposition to this holy and divine communion through sin.[5]

Human action, accordingly, does not build up *communio*: indeed, it may even cause damage to it, if God wants to give it to man.

Hans Urs von Balthasar describes it in a rather similar way:

> *Communio* is the *Ur*-mystery: namely, that God should out of his own free love share all the goods of his love with one who is not God.[6]

If *communio* is the sharing in the life of God himself, then it necessarily eludes a precise definition.

[4] Cf. W. Kasper, "Die Kirche als Sakrament der Einheit", *Internationale katholische Zeitschrift* 16 (1987): 2–8, here 5.

[5] Origen, Hom. 4, 4, In Lev.

[6] Hans Urs von Balthasar, *Theodramatik*, vol. 2. (Einsiedeln, 1976), 114.

Sharing in God's life cannot be reduced to a concise linguistic formula. It is revealed in many situations in the life of Christians. A description of the situations in which the early Church made use of this concept can, however, help to elucidate its meaning.

3. *Communio* Through the Eucharist and "Communion Letters"

The first fact that strikes us is that, for the early Fathers of the Church, this sharing in the life of God was accomplished through the sacraments. The Eucharist in particular was regarded as the source and causation of Communion in the Church. This is how it is presented, for instance, in the *Didaskalie* dating to the third century:

> When a [nonlocal] bishop arrives, he should sit with the [diocesan] bishop and receive the same honor as him. And you, [diocesan] bishop, request him to give an address to your people. . . . At the celebration of the Eucharist he should himself speak the words of the canon. But if he is polite and wishes to let you have the honor, and therefore does not wish [to consecrate], he should [at least] speak [the words of consecration] over the chalice.[7]

---

[7] Ed. Funk, II, 58, 2.

The Church's Communion was thus expressed by the common form of the eucharistic sacrifice.

Corresponding with this view of Communion is a usage already found in a letter written by Irenaeus of Lyons to Pope Victor about the controversy over the Easter festival in the second century. He mentions the custom whereby the bishop of Rome would separate a portion of the consecrated host during Holy Mass; this would then be preserved for the next celebration of the Eucharist. After an appropriate rite, other portions were sent to all the priests in the various districts of the city. They in turn placed the particles of the host in the chalice as an addition before the priestly greeting of peace. The practice was a way of testifying that "the same sacrifice, the same Eucharist, the same communion was celebrated" at all liturgical gatherings.[8]

Bishops too testified among themselves to interdiocesan *communio* by sharing the Body of the Lord among one another in the Eucharist. Many liturgical texts mention this practice with a view to the consecration of priests and bishops until far into the Middle Ages.

The *communio* of the Eucharist, in short, formed the basis of communion in the early Church.[9] In

[8] Eusebius, *Hist. eccl.*, bk. 5, chap. 24, n. 15: SC 41, 70–71.

[9] On the following see L. Hertling, "Communio und Primat—Kirche und Papsttum in der christliche Antike", *Una Sancta* 17 (1962): 91–125.

times of schism, therefore, each Christian belonged to the community in which he received Holy Communion. This conviction led to some odd results. Thus, the heretical patriarch Macedonius of Constantinople used force to oblige the Catholics opposed to him to receive Holy Communion from him: he ordered that their mouths be forcibly opened and the Body of the Lord thus administered to them.[10]

The view expressed here persisted for a long time. Even at the beginning of the seventh century Sophronius tells us of an Alexandrian monophysite who wanted to become Catholic. Since he was afraid of his fellow-sectarians, he secretly received Holy Communion in the Catholic basilica of the Mother of God. The matter was discovered on the Catholic side and the conversion finalized without further ado.[11]

Such a procedure may seem to us today a bit mechanical, even magical. Yet in this way expression was given to the fact that the eucharistic celebration and the receiving of Holy Communion in it form a clearer bond of *communio* than words or symbolic deeds, a fact that should be considered by all those who today accuse the Roman Catholic Church of ecumenical obstruction because she does not permit intercommunion.

[10] PG 47, 325.
[11] PG 87/3, 3460ff.

Apart from the *communio* that had its roots in the joint celebration of the Eucharist, there was another form of ecclesial communion in the early Church. This at first seems to have had a purely bourgeois or administrative character: a kind of membership card certifying belonging to the Faith. When a priest or a layman in the early Church went on a journey, he took with him an affidavit, a kind of passport, from his bishop. This gave him great advantages. The holder of such a "passport" was welcomed as a brother by Christians wherever he went and given free hospitality. That the document in question was more than a form of travel insurance is suggested by the name given to it: it was called a "communion letter". Apart from their practical and economic significance, these letters were also an important means of strengthening communion between the bishops and between the local churches.

Each bishop, or at any rate each individual church of any note, drew up a list of the most important churches throughout the world with which it was in *communio*. This list served as a register of addresses that could be used when "passports" had to be issued. Conversely, the "passports" of visitors to the church in question could be checked against it.

Augustine once used this procedure to expose a bishop associated with the Donatist heresy in the course of a public disputation. The Donatist boasted that he was in no way separated from the true Church; that he lived in *communio* with the whole Church. Augustine challenged this claim by asking him if he could issue letters to the churches Augustine wished to put to him (such as Corinth, Ephesus or Alexandria). The Donatist had to backtrack: his letters were accepted in none of these churches. [12]

Communio between individual churches also implied the bond of unity between bishops and faithful in each of them. Each of these churches should be conceived not as a hierarchical pyramid, but as an embodiment of *communio*. Cyprian writes to his church from his hiding place that he didn't want to make any final decisions at this time, since he had resolved right from the start to do nothing without the advice of the clergy and the agreement of the people. [13] Yet there can be no doubt that, already in the early Church, the bishop was sole master in the house of the diocese. He combined in himself the biblical teaching of personal leadership, in just the same way as the role of the bishop is defined by the Second Vatican Council, which affirms that the bishop presides in God's stead over his flock in the role of teacher of doctrine, minister of sacred worship and holder of office in the government of the diocese (cf. *Lumen Gentium*, no. 20). In the early Church everything

[12] CSEL 34, 111.
[13] CSEL 3/2, 512.

depended on the bishop, and everything went through his hand, right down to the details of alms for the poor. Yet alongside him the clergy also played an important role. Without the clergy, whom the bishop addressed as *Conpresbyteroi* and *Condiakonoi*, the bishop decided nothing. The people too played a participatory role, even in the appointment of a lector.[14]

This cooperation in the local church was once again rooted in the eucharistic *communio*. Saint Ignatius wrote to the Philadelphians from Antioch:

> Be zealous, then, in the observance of the Eucharist. For there is one flesh of our Lord, Jesus Christ, and one chalice that brings union in his blood. There is one altar, as there is one bishop with the priests and deacons, who are many fellow-workers. And so, whatever you do, let it be done in the name of God.[15]

Precisely because of this dependence on the eucharistic sacrifice and ultimately on the Lord himself, *communio* cannot be encompassed by or reduced to a social and organizational structure. As the bishops stressed in the final report of the Extraordinary Synod in 1985: "The ecclesiology of communion cannot be reduced to mere ques-

[14] Hertling, op. cit., 107.

[15] St. Ignatius of Antioch, Letter to the Philadelphians (no. 4), in *The Fathers of the Church: The Apostolic Fathers* (New York, 1948), 114.

tions of organization or questions concerning mere powers" (C 1). For if the idea of *communio* were to be embodied in hierarchical sociopolitical organizations or structures of shared responsibility, it would be falsified at its very heart: *communio* can become a reality not through human planning but only when the individual Christian—be he bishop, priest or layman—submits himself to God's sovereignty over him. God's Spirit will accordingly maintain his place in the Church only if the battle of the Apostle of the Gentiles against division and fossilization be constantly fought anew.

4. *Communio* and the Universal Church

The political model of absolutism is thus ruled out for the episcopal government of the individual church. And this is due not only to the fundamental differences we have pointed out between political and ecclesial strivings toward unity. The wider unity of the Church is also incompatible with an absolutist system of episcopal government: the individual bishop's membership of the world episcopate and its presupposition, the correlation between particular and universal Church, repudiate the thesis that the unity of the Church is the result of the federation of more or less independent local churches. Dioceses are not monads.

Each must be a living cell, so that it is "open on all sides through the bond of communion, for its identity as a church can be preserved only through this openness, through this interlacing in the net of communion of the Church herself".[16] This is something that an attentive reading can already recognize in the very mode of address of the Apostle Paul. Paul does not address himself simply to the church in Corinth but to "the Church of God which is at Corinth" (1 Cor 1:2). In his Letter to the Romans, he similarly speaks of "the church at Cenchreae" (Rom 16:1). Yet it is always the same Church of God in these and many other places.

During the early Christian period, if a bishop wanted to show his own belonging to the Church's *communio*, he had only to communicate with a church that itself formed part of it.[17] It was enough therefore for him to communicate, for instance, with the bishop of Gubbio, Calama or Cyzicus; if these bishops were included in the general *communio*, they could also transmit it to those communicating with them. Yet as soon as it became doubtful whether the bishop of Cyzicus belonged to the Universal Church, then *communio* with him brought no legitimization. He then had

---

[16] Cf. J. Ratzinger, "Die pastoral Implikationen der Lehre von der Kollegialität der Bischöfe", in *Das neue Volk Gottes* (Düsseldorf, 1969), 201–24, here 206.

[17] Cf. Hertling, op. cit., 112ff.

to prove in other ways that he really formed part of the *communio*. But how could he do so?

An important criterion to this end was, first, that a large number of dioceses testified to *communio* with him. When a bishop lived in *communio* with many hundred bishops throughout the world, his *communio* would *ipso facto* be the right one, even if one or two bishops denied it to him. This criterion was especially adopted by the Greeks as a proof of their *communio*; Athanasius, Basil and others could point to practically the whole map of the Roman Empire in enumerating the churches with which they were in communion and in thus showing that they belonged to the true *communio*.

Another criterion was *communio* with the earliest churches, i.e., with those founded by the Apostles. This method was especially adopted by the Africans in their dispute with the Donatists. Irenaeus and Tertullian also sought to vindicate themselves by this method. For, depending on circumstance, a large number of bishops might already have gravitated into the heretical camp; in this case, the quantitative criterion—the large number of churches with which a bishop was in *communio*—was a weak proof.

The above criteria of *communio* were also applicable if clearly defined relationships reigned. However, if a bishop wanted to seek absolute assurance, he would then appeal to *communio* with

Rome. Rome stood at the top of the list of the key churches. A church that stood in *communio* with Rome *ipso facto* had *communio* with all other Catholic churches in the world. This was asserted by Optatus, bishop of Milevis: "Damasus was followed [as bishop of Rome] by Siricius, who is today our colleague [in the episcopate], with whom [i.e., through whom] the whole world agrees in the exchange of letters in the communion of a single *communio*." And Augustine writes: "Carthage had [in Cyprian's time] a bishop of no small reputation, who did not need to fear even a host of enemies, since he knew that he was united through communion letters both with the Roman Church, in which the primacy of the apostolic see has always been in force, and also with the other countries." And Irenaeus, in his *Adversus haereses*, writes: "All churches must find themselves [in communion] together with this Church [i.e., the Church of Rome] on account of its quite particular preeminence."[18]

In the view of the early Fathers of the Church, the theological truth of *communio* did not merely contain a constant proof of its theocentricity, a proof that it is the product not of any human effort but grows from communion with God himself. At the same time it was a guiding idea for the Church's understanding of herself. Thanks to a

---

[18] Referred to by Hertling, op. cit.

belief in *communio*, the Church also gained an ever clearer idea about her building up and about the special mission entrusted to the bishop of Rome for the preservation of the Church in unity and truth. For the theological truth of *communio* prevented the Church from developing into, or from conceiving herself as, a federation of separated provinces, territorial churches or cultural spheres of influence.

Of course, the Church right from the outset inevitably lived in the individual church. It was established in particular geographical locations and gathered together people characterized by different historical and environmental backgrounds. Yet the local church was not like a fortress that could shut itself off from the surrounding world. It would be a historical illusion and a theological error to suppose that it could, if it wanted, erect boundaries against theological currents and pastoral impulses. Our Church is the *Catholica*: in its worldwide multiplicity it is *one*. Pascal penned the epigram: "The variety that does not combine to form unity, is confusion; the unity that is not dependent on variety, is tyranny."[19] The maxim was admittedly prompted by the attack that the French writer mounted against the papacy, yet it does have its wider justification. And in contrast to what Pascal says, the See of Peter does guarantee

---

[19] Blaise Pascal, *Pensées*.

the Church in history of a unity that is dependent on variety and of a unity that ensures scope for the new.

An instance of this is provided by the controversy over the mendicant orders in the Middle Ages.[20] I would like briefly to dwell on this dispute, which subjected the new foundations of the Franciscans and the Dominicans to very severe scrutiny. For it enables us to gain a better understanding of the link between papacy and *communio*.

5. Papacy and *Communio*

On the threshold of the thirteenth century, secular priests and monks coexisted peaceably together in their local churches. Those in religious orders limited themselves to the fields of pastoral work allocated to them and left intact the competence of the pastoral clergy. Yet this peaceful coexistence was rudely disturbed by the religious movements called into life by Francis and Dominic. Monks unattached to a particular monastery, monks without any fixed residence, began to wander the length and breadth of Europe. They preached wherever the spirit urged them. They

[20] On what follows, see J. Ratzinger, "Zum Einfluss des Bettelordenstreites auf die Entwicklung der Primatslehre", in *Das neue Volk Gottes* (Düsseldorf, 1969), 49–71.

had no benefices, no revenue, but depended for their livelihood on the charity of the Christians they met on their way. By word of mouth and personal witness they brought the Gospel of Jesus Christ so much to life that their following among the people was great. In so doing, they stood the ecclesial and economic order of the Middle Ages on its head.

1. The locally circumscribed right to pastoral care of parish priests and bishops was transgressed or ignored by these intrusive friars who belonged to no parish, no diocese. The generosity of the faithful was naturally directed at those who, like the mendicant friars, aroused more sympathy in their poverty and zeal than did the well-provided and comfortable secular clergy.

2. The mendicant orders avoided—unintentionally—the whole system of benefices and church livings as such. For they propagated a form of life that did not concern itself with providing for the next day, but awaited all their needs to come unbidden from the heavenly Father. They were thus free from the material bond with the house of a religious order. Only the spiritual bond with the community and, at a higher level, with the *minister generalis* had any weight.

The breakdown of hierarchical frontiers caused by the mendicant orders led to a situation in which ministers were active on all sides who were provided with no episcopal brief or episcopal authority, but were emissaries of a minister-general who claimed to be answerable to none but the Pope. This mean that a group of priests was now active throughout the Christian world who were immediately subordinate to the Pope, without the interposition of a locally dependent prelate.[21]

The centralism fostered by the mendicant orders in this way also had its repercussions on the idea of the Church of the faithful as a whole: the See of Peter was given a stronger image.

These developments did not go unchallenged. The opponents of the mendicant friars attacked not only them but the new centralism they had instigated. William of Saint-Amour, a bitter opponent of the mendicant orders, appealed to the authority of Dionysius the Pseudo-Areopagite in support of his attack. He interpreted this Church Father as essentially antipapalist and demanded a kind of principle of subsidiarity for the spiritual powers: as if the episcopal power could not be bypassed or overridden by the Pope, as was in effect happening in the case of the permission granted to the centrally organized mendicant friars to preach and hear confessions. Nor did William of Saint-Amour resort to false arguments in his support for the particular church: he stressed papal fallibility. It was also alleged he had called for a general council against the Pope.

[21] Ibid., 55.

In this situation, the mendicant orders came to the defense of the See of Peter and at the same time fought for their own rights. Saint Bonaventure was one of their most significant spokesmen. His central argument was that the Church herself had canonized Francis and Dominic and had thus endorsed the new mendicant form of life they had prescribed for their friars. The Church as the People of God could not err. The decisive factor in this process had finally proved to be the Pope himself, whose authority would have been put into doubt if the attack on the mendicant orders had carried the day. And so Bonaventure means the bishop of Rome himself when he appears to the Holy Church:

> You, Holy Roman Church, you, a new Esther, who stand uplifted over the peoples as mother of all Churches, as queen and mistress in matters of faith and morals, you are beseeched full of trust by your poor community, powerfully and righteously to defend now as a queen those whom you procreated as a mother and suckled as a nurse. . . . "Stand up", Holy Mother, and "do justice" (Esther 3:6), for it is your own affair if the order of the poor Friars Minor properly fulfills the Gospel truth; it is *your* affair if its form of life, which you have called good, deviates from the truth. Therefore, if this holy form of life be accused of error, it is *you* who will be accused of the error by virtue of the approval of it you granted, and you, hitherto mistress of the truth, will thus be accused of the

approval of error, and mocked by the presumption of the moderns, as if you knew nothing about divine and human right."[22]

From the self-defense of the mendicant orders, the Church received renewed spiritual impetus for spreading the Gospel; the Universal Church remained no abstract idea but became, through the exertions of the mendicant friars, a tangible reality at the level of the local churches, with the result that the *Catholica* won renewed missionary strength worldwide.

And it was at this moment that the papacy showed herself to be the guarantor of spiritual resurgence. Quite the reverse to the fears expressed by Pascal, she did not react in a repressive way but held in check the absolutist tendencies of the local churches. Cardinal Ratzinger presciently points out in his article *Pluralismus als Frage an Kirche und Theologie* that the two major thrusts that brought the doctrine of primacy to its full expression—namely, the contest in the West over the freedom of the Church from the state under Gregory VII (d. 1057), and the conflict over the mendicant orders in the thirteenth century—derived their impetus not from unitarian interest but from the dynamic of pluralist demands. That the Gregorian reform and the recognition of the mendicant orders are, now as ever, of the greatest actuality

---

[22] Ibid., 62.

needs no demonstration. Cardinal Ratzinger declares:

> Only the Universal Church can ensure the separation of the particular church from state and society. Today too, we are similarly experiencing the phenomenon of apostolic movements coming "from below" and transcending the local church: movements in which new charisms are emerging and animating the local pastoral ministry. Today too, such movements, which cannot be derived from the episcopal principle, find their theological and practical justification in primacy.[23]

It is thus not possible to present, as the Italian theologian B. Forte has attempted to do in a study on the laity,[24] the lay associations, movements and missionary activity in the Church totally divorced from the perspective of the Universal Church. Forte makes a fundamental mistake in limiting his analysis to the "local church" and in claiming "primacy" for it, and not for the Universal Church, ultimately on psychological and sociological grounds. As a logical consequence he attributes no theological relevance to the papacy for the formulation of the question and, in the course of his argument, concerns himself with it only once (p. 74). He raises once again, as the antipapal-

---

[23] *Forum katholischer Theologie* 2 (1986): 81–96, here 91.

[24] B. Forte, *Laicato e laicità: Saggi ecclesiologici* (Casale Monferrato, 1986).

ist opponents of the mendicant orders had done in the thirteenth century, the claims of the principle of subsidiarity (p. 72), without even mentioning the difficulties raised about the possible use of this principle in the Church by the Extraordinary Synod of Bishops in 1985; difficulties that led the Synodal Fathers to recommend a study of the question whether the principle of subsidiarity "that has force in human society can be applied in the Church, and at what level and in what sense such application could or ought to take place" (C 8c).

If we follow Forte's line of thought, we find ourselves faced with a situation in which the concept of *communio* is reduced to a meaningless phrase, which means nothing more than a kind of diocesan comformity: division is to be presented purely at the administrative level. *Communio* is divested of its divine source and atrophied into an administrative procedure: it is no longer seen as a gift that enables the faithful to share the meeting with the crucified Lord in the celebration of the Eucharist, and that constantly challenges them to confront themselves anew with God's will.

6. *Communio* and the Consecrated Ministry

The resolute turning to the papacy must dispel any impartial person's concern that the theological truth of *communio* is here used in opposition to the consecrated ministry in the Church. That would be a fatal misunderstanding. On the occasion of the Synod of Bishops on the role of the laity, many members of the Church demanded, somewhat unreflectingly, the final democratization of the Church. Not without reproach, they maintained that the laity should itself decide on its participation in the Church's mission. The Second Vatican Council, after all, had—they argued—made it clear once and for all that, in the Church too, all power springs from the people, the people of God. Even bishops wondered aloud what possible meaning and justification a synod of bishops on the theme of the laity could have.

It is not the promotion of this trend but *communio* as fruit and dynamic impetus of the Holy Spirit that needs to be kept in view, and this is something that the Church's ordained ministry must also take into consideration. Cardinal Wojtyla said at the synod of bishops in 1969: "[*Communio*] is the kind of unity that can be achieved ever more deeply and fully amid a multiplicity and diversity of believers by means of Communion."[25]

Anyone who appeals to the authority of Saint Paul cannot call for basic democracy for the Church. For the message he spells out with all the

[25] K. *Wojtyla e il Sinodo dei Vescovi* (Città del Vaticano, 1980), 340.

authority of a leader elected by God runs too clearly and unmistakably through all his letters. He judges self-styled charismatic prophets harshly. In the already cited initial chapters of the First Letter to the Corinthians, he takes issue with those who think they are appealing to the Spirit but who are in reality appealing to themselves (1 Cor 3:18). His words here are unusually sharp and plain-spoken:

> I will come to you soon, if the Lord wills, and I will find out not the talk of these arrogant people but their power. For the kingdom of God does not consist in talk but in power. What do you wish? Shall I come to you with a rod, or with love in a spirit of gentleness?
>
> — 1 Cor 4:19–21

Whoever claims to be filled with the Spirit will not want to stand on the sidelines of the Church. He will be enabled by the power of this same Spirit to recognize that the commands of the Apostle, by virtue of the full authority vested in him, are "a command of the Lord" (1 Cor 14:37). Paul himself therefore does not fight shy of the appeal: "Do not quench the spirit, do not despise prophesying" (1 Th 5:19). And the Decree on the Ministry and Life of Priests of the Second Vatican Council admonishes the pastors of the Church:

> While trying the spirits if they be of God, they [the priests] must discover with faith, recognize with

joy and foster with diligence the many and varied charismatic gifts of the laity, whether these be of a humble or more exalted kind. Among the other gifts of God that are found abundantly among the faithful, special attention ought to be devoted to those graces by which a considerable number of people are attracted to greater heights of the spiritual life. Priests should also be confident in giving lay people charge of duties in the service of the Church, giving them freedom and opportunity for activity and even inviting them, when opportunity occurs, to take the initiative in undertaking projects of their own.[26]

[26] *Presbyterorum ordinis,* no. 9.

ACKNOWLEDGMENTS

The chapters this book originally appeared in the following sources:

I "Der spirituelle Aufbruch in der Weltkirche", in *Internationale katholische Zeitschrift* 16 (1987): 49–66.

II "Da San Francesco a Charles de Foucauld: Gesù come unico modello della vita cristiana", in *Osservatore Romano*, 4/5 October 1982.

III "Erfahrung als Hilfe zum Glauben", in *Internationale katholische Zeitschrift* 11 (1982): 281–93; English translation (revised for the present book) in *Center Journal* published by the Center for Christian Studies, Notre Dame University, Indiana, Winter 1982, pp. 57–79.

IV *Neuzeitliche Demokratie und das gemeinsame Priestertum aller Gläubigen*, paper given to the plenary assembly of the Pontifical Council for the Laity 1980 (unpublished).

V "Die *communio* in der Kirche: Für ein theozentrisches Verständnis von Einheit", Italian translation in *I Movimenti nella Chiesa, Atti del 2, colloquio Internazionale*, Milan, 1987.